Anthropology & Education

The major objective of this series is to make the knowledge and perspective of anthropology available to educators and their students. It is hoped and believed, however, that it will also prove valuable to those in other professions and in the several disciplines that comprise the behavioral ciences.

In recent years some educators have discovered that anthropology has much to offer the areas of professional training and educational theory and practice. In its cross-cultural comparisons of human behavior and in its inductive, empirical method of analysis is found a conceptual freshness that is intellectually liberating.

Actually, there are four major areas of anthropological theory which have direct relevance for education. These are the transmission of culture and learning processes; the regularities of behavior and belief which we call culture; the ways in which individuals group themselves for the accomplishment of communal purposes, from which comes organization theory; and the processes by which transformations occur in human behavior and groupings which can be explained by a theory of change. In addition, there are the subject-matter areas of child rearing; community and the relationships among institutions within it; the rites of passage; the cultural categories of social class, ethnic group, age, grading, and sex; and others.

These several areas of theory and substance provide a rich source for this series. For example, there are plans for analyses of the relevance of anthropology to each educational specialty, such as administration, guidance, and curriculum. In another direction, the perspective and method of such areas as social anthropology, applied anthropology, and linguistics in relation to education will be examined. Several studies about educational activities which use anthropological research methods and concepts will appear. Other subject areas for the series include the culture of childhood, comparative educational systems, methods of research, and the exemplification of anthropological theory in subject-matter organization. It is believed that the availability of such a storehouse of knowledge in the several volumes in this series will contribute immensely to the further improvement of our educational system.

Solon T. Kimball, *General Editor*

Perspectives
from
Anthropology

RACHEL REESE SADY

TEACHERS COLLEGE PRESS
Teachers College, Columbia University

Foreword

In recent years there has been increasing interest on the part of educators and others in the subject matter and approach of anthropology. Those who have acquired this new awareness have often suffered confusion and frustration when attempting to find an account
which would describe without technical terms or professional argot
what it is that anthropologists do and what anthropology is all about.
Although many have profited who have read accounts of tribal or
peasant peoples or who have delved into one of the relatively few
books written for the intelligent and curious public, it is still difficult to find any one volume which presents an overview of this field
for the general reader. The fact is that most anthropologists write
for their colleagues.

There is need for a book which explains and interprets what anthropology is about. That is the purpose of *Perspectives from Anthropology*. Its author, Dr. Rachel Reese Sady, conveys to us the
intellectual orientation which distinguishes the anthropological approach to the study of man. We are introduced to the subject by a
description of the variety of activities in which anthropologists engage while gathering their data in the field and an explanation of
how this information contributes to answering the questions that
anthropologists ask. Dr. Sady examines briefly the significance of
anthropology for education. From there she moves to the heart of
the problem—the anthropological perspective and how it is reflected
in concepts about the diversity of the ways of man as well as the universals of human behavior. Finally, she writes about the meaning
and values of anthropology both for the world we live in and for
ourselves.

It is inevitable that an author's writings reflect something of his
background, and so it is with Dr. Sady. Her graduate work in an-

thropology was at the University of Chicago and in Mexico just prior to the Second World War. She applied her skills during the war years in the Community Analysis Section of the War Relocation Authority, which was responsible for administering the centers in which the Japanese Americans evacuated from the West Coast were interned, and later, on the staff of President Truman's historic Committee on Civil Rights. More recently she has completed assignments for the Anthropology Curriculum Study Project financed by the National Science Foundation, and what may be of even greater importance, as a mother and citizen she has been fully involved in the educational system of the community in which she lives. These roles exemplify the scientific and humanitarian aspects of life, both of which are combined in the perspective of anthropology.

Solon T. Kimball

Acknowledgement

Acknowledgement is primarily due the many men and women who have done the field work, fashioned the methods, and built the theories that have crystallized into what is called an "anthropological point of view." In the body of the book, particular examples are credited to the anthropologists and sociologists from whose work they are drawn. I would like to thank for their suggestions and criticisms of the manuscript Solon T. Kimball, Malcolm Collier, Robert Rittner and Emil J. Sady.

Rachel Reese Sady

Contents

Perspectives
from
Anthropology

1

Introduction

The bond between anthropology and education is recent and, although already quite firm, still requires understanding and accommodation on both sides. This book attempts to strengthen the bond by presenting one version of "the anthropological point of view" to those who are involved with the schools or interested in education. This version stresses the perspectives from anthropology that seem most directly relevant to educational goals and processes. It is neither a text for an introductory course in anthropology nor a history of the development of anthropological theory; rather it is a synthesis of ideas from anthropology that are pertinent to the tasks of the schools today.

After a panoramic view of what anthropology is and what anthropologists do, the perspectives are presented in two groups: those that recognize the great diversity of the ways of man and those that emphasize their essential unity. Anthropological methods, concepts, and data are discussed in the context of what is unique and what is universal in culture. The concluding chapter indicates the value of an anthropological point of view for understanding not only other peoples but also ourselves.

Anthropology and Anthropologists

AT WORK IN THE FIELD

If we imagine anthropologists at work in the field, many different scenes could come to mind. For example, one might be pictured moving among the people of a remote tribe, mapping the village, canvas-

1

sing the dwellings, finding out who lives in each household and what they call each other. Or he might be seen with the villagers as they go about their daily chores, noting how the work is divided, or as they attend a religious ceremony or some other special event. He is watching, listening, often asking questions, and always jotting down what he has seen and heard in a notebook. In contrast, another anthropologist might be found in the midst of the hubbub of a large city neighborhood, visiting members of a particular ethnic or age group, attending their social affairs and meetings, observing how they behave with one another in both casual and formal situations. Like his colleague in the distant village, he is watching and listening, asking questions, and recording in his notebook.

Still another might be found interviewing an elder, a man full of years and experience, and filling the now more obvious notebook with what his informant tells him of an old, almost vanished way of life—of how the world looked when the elder was young, of what he learned when he was growing up. Or the anthropologist may be seen asking particular questions of a whole series of informants, perhaps systematically noting the answers on special forms.

Other anthropologists at work in the field could be observed sitting with informants as they speak in their own language, recording what is said on tape or on paper, with particular symbols standing for particular sounds, taking down word lists, longer expressions, or texts of whole myths and other lore. Others could be found in the countryside, carefully removing layers of debris from a plotted site, sifting the crumbling dirt for potsherds or other remnants of a past life; or they might be surveying an earthen floor, noting the distinct coloration of the soil that might mean a post was once sunk here or a campfire once blazed over there. Thousands of miles away another anthropologist might be engaged in the more glamorous but no more relevant task of opening a tomb where well-preserved ceramics, intricately-worked gold and turquoise, and other rich objects attest to the former importance of the grave's occupant.

Glimpses of still other anthropologists in the field could find them at such diverse pursuits as prying old bones from earth and rock, measuring living peoples, drawing blood samples, recording genealogies, or quietly observing from a vantage in the bush for hours on end the social activities of a troop of baboons or some other of man's relatives among the primates.

In all of these widely varied professional activities, the anthropologists are doing essentially the same thing. They are collecting the raw material of their science: data on man and his activities. Since all peoples live in certain environments and in certain groups, this information includes how humans behave in relation to their natural environment, by making technological and other adaptations to climate and terrain, and in relation to each other—how they are organized to conduct life activities. The anthropologists are all concerned with human behavior whether their particular "field" is the territory of a hunting and gathering band, an agricultural village, or an urban neighborhood; and also whether they are observing people in a small group, a large community, or a still larger area with a common culture. And of course it is still behavior that interests them whether they can actually see the people working, playing, eating, and responding to one another, or can only hear about how people used to do these things in times gone by, or guess about such activities from clues discovered in places where people used to live. Even those anthropologists most concerned with the biology and origin of man, and therefore with his relationship with both earlier and present-day primates, are ultimately concerned with answering behavioral questions.

THE SUBJECT

Anthropology is the study of man and his way of life. This definition may seem so encompassing as to be practically boundless, but anthropologists value it precisely because of its scope which allows them to deal with the whole of man in all of his relationships. At the same time they are not overwhelmed by the magnitude of their task because they recognize, realistically, that in the history of anthropology certain approaches, problems, and methods have developed that pattern their activity. The anthropologist is in a comfortable position: anthropological tradition points out the various pathways he can take, and the broad scope of the field allows him to follow them wherever they lead, through new territory or across disciplinary boundaries to work with geneticists, sociologists, historians, psychologists—or educators.

The preceding thumbnail descriptions of anthropologists at work in the field reflect some of the kinds of anthropology that are practiced. Usually two main branches are recognized: *physical anthropology* and *cultural anthropology*. *Physical anthropology* is concerned with the origin and evolution of man and his biological adaptation to his world; the subject is approached through evolutionary theory, the fossil record, and comparative anatomical and physiological studies.

Cultural anthropology includes all those diversified anthropological studies that are concerned with man's cultural or learned behavior. Some anthropologists use the term *social anthropology* almost synonymously, but others reserve it specifically for attempts to arrive at generalizations or laws about social systems. *Archaeology* is the study of past cultures and *ethnology* is the study of recent cultures, usually distinguished by its interest in historical relationships from *ethnography*, which is purely descriptive and serves as the basis for both culture history and social generalization. *Linguistics* is a special kind of anthropology that is cultural since language is a cultural phenomenon, but set apart because of the unique nature of the subject and the specialized methods and techniques used in studying it.

All of these subfields are overlapping, as can be expected from their common core of interest. So are cultural studies that emphasize a particular aspect of human organization and are called by their practitioners *psychological, economic,* or *political anthropology.* The unity of anthropology may be so evident in particular studies as to defy easy pigeonholing of them into subbranches. Even the distinction between physical and cultural anthropology cannot be made as easily now as it could be earlier, before physical anthropologists discovered the important role of culture itself in the biological evolution of man and applied themselves to understanding the complex interrelationships involved.

Anthropology is characteristically concerned with human behavior and the social and cultural forces that affect it and are affected by it. The study has focussed broadly on two closely connected problems: how cultures have developed and how societies are organized. As indicated by the preceding descriptions of anthropologists in the field, anthropology is also characterized—almost diagnostically—by its reliance on observations made in the field, the raw data for analysis and meaningful synthesis. How this data is handled is another unifying characteristic of the study of man.

THE METHOD

The basic methodological approach of anthropology, inherited from natural history where it was used successfully to explain biological phenomena, is to collect observations in the field, classify this data, and compare it with similarly collected and classified data in order to identify significant differences and similarities. Anthropologists relish speaking of "raw data" and a "rigorous methodology," and of the insights "emerging from the data themselves." Although the data are not quite as "raw" and the method is not as "rigorous" as such descriptions imply, anthropologists do make special attempts to minimize personal and cultural bias, to see objectively in a particular community or event whatever there is to see, and to record as much of it as possible without regard to preconceptions. Even so, the anthropologist cannot be a sponge soaking up data indiscriminately. He may or may not have a specific problem in mind that he wants to investigate, but he most certainly is aware of various concepts, specific ways of classifying and thinking about data that are current in anthropology. When he sits down to order and analyze his field data, he searches for significant relationships between his assorted facts, and he does so with reference to selected concepts, or else develops new, more satisfactory ones.

The material thus developed from an analysis of the field data is then available for cross-cultural comparisons. Not all of it is so used—anthropologists accuse themselves of sometimes repeating the obvious or belaboring the trivial. But comparison with our own culture is always implicit, and fruitful comparisons with ours and the whole range of cultures are frequently explicit.

To sum up, anthropology seeks to understand man in general through the study of man in particular cases. Its subject is mankind, its data are derived from observation, and its method is comparative.

The Relevance of Anthropology to Education

The schools have one foot in the past and one in the future, and of necessity the first one is the more firmly planted. The pedagogical purpose is to teach skills, impart knowledge, develop abilities, and support values in order to turn children into good adult citizens who can get along in the world and at the same time improve it. This involves passing on solid blocks of cultural tradition, yet encouraging innovation in a rapidly changing and ever more complex and intimate world. This is a mammoth task, and the schools need all the help they can get. Anthropology can contribute a point of view that relates to both cultural tradition and cultural change and that is well-supported by concrete evidence.

THE POINT OF VIEW

The anthropological point of view is humanistic in its concern for the well-being of man and scientific in its attempt to see its subject objectively. This combination of the compassionate and the dispassionate greatly widens the usual framework for understanding man and his works. The widened frame contains a paradox: man is one entity, with common cultural as well as biological characteristics, and yet man possesses a far-ranging diversity of unique cultures. Anthropologists suggest the resolution of this paradox through understanding the various cultures both on their own terms and in relation to a common humanity. This involves a great deal more than a simple listing of apparent ways in which each culture is unique and all cultures are similar. The most diverse kinds of behavior can stem from universal needs and qualities, and seeming similarities can overlie very real and deep-seated differences. To understand the ways of man a whole series of interrelationships must be investigated: how cultures are patterned, how societies function, how culture is transmitted, and how culture changes. Cultural diversity and universality are not opposing images of man; they are intricately interwoven strands in the same tapestry. One must occur in the company of the other. The paradox is only apparent.

TEACHING ANTHROPOLOGY

Communicating these perspectives about mankind to students is vital to contemporary education, but it can only be successful if accompanied by a body of knowledge, by some of the specific descriptions and analyses from which the perspectives have been distilled. Concepts and data together should add to students' abilities to live with humane and practical purpose in a world populated by diverse peoples.

In the classroom there is no particular need to label as anthropology any of the ideas or facts taught, although sometimes the word with its exotic connotations seems to stimulate interest. The concepts and facts can be scattered throughout the substance of any social studies course. The ideas themselves will vary in relevancy to particular courses or fit more comfortably with some curriculum approaches than with others. The particular information used for illustration here is chosen arbitrarily from a vast ethnographical literature. In most cases other examples from each teacher's own living and reading experience can be substituted for it.

LOOKING AT EDUCATION ANTHROPOLOGICALLY

At the beginning of this introduction anthropologists were described in various surroundings at different tasks. One scene was not sketched: the anthropologist sitting in the classroom or walking around the school, listening to and watching students, teachers, and school administrators, talking with parents in the school community—still with notebook in hand, still the participant-observer in this more familiar "field." This scene represents another area of cooperation between anthropology and education. In this area the methods and concepts of anthropology are applied to education as to any other social system. The same procedure that helps us understand other cultures and the social units of strange societies—collecting raw data and analyzing it according to certain concepts—can help us understand our own culture and its schools. Every analysis of a school system that describes its stated and its implied goals, the ways individuals within the system communicate and cooperate to accomplish these goals, and the actual results, becomes a case study potentially comparable with other such studies. The teacher who seeks to impart some anthropological facts and concepts in the classroom can perhaps also start to look at that classroom and what goes on in it as part of a social system and part of a cultural process. Both applications of anthropology in education—teaching it and using it—have the same core.

2

The Diversity of Cultures

The English explorer John Ross, while leading an expedition to the Arctic in 1818, came upon a hunting party of Polar Eskimo. According to Ross' account, although he and his men had not believed that Eskimo lived so far north, it was the Eskimo who were the more astounded at the encounter.[1] They had apparently believed until that moment that their people were the only ones in the world, a world that was completely bound by snow and ice. They did not call themselves *Eskimo* (which is an Indian word referring to the Eskimo's diet of raw flesh), but *Innuit*, which means simply "men" or "people."

Many other groups living on every continent similarly have only one name for themselves and for people in general. How many of them once thought that they were the only people in the only world is hard to say. It is plain, however, that there is a strong tendency for every society to consider its own way of life, if demonstrably not the only one, at least the natural one. Such ethnocentrism is not limited to small, isolated groups. The ancient Greeks and Romans were so ethnocentric that they lumped all other peoples together as barbarians. Herodotus described the customs of peoples he visited on his travels as being distinct from each other as well as from Greek civilization, but his compatriots thought him a liar when he reported such differences—or else mad for being interested in them.

Such extreme ethnocentric views did not give way to even an interest in other people's customs until vast new worlds were discovered and explored and the antiquities of the old world were excavated and investigated. At first explorers, then missionaries, government agents, and others wrote of the strange ways of the people they found themselves among. This information, added to the data on past cultures that historians and classical archaeologists were compiling, presented an overwhelming picture of cultural diversity in both time and space. Anthropologists used all of this material, and still do, but the young science was not established on a firm base until its acolytes left their armchairs for the field. Now the extraordinary diversity of the world's cultures is documented in whole libraries of ethnographies, and the process of documentation continues as anthropologists strive to describe unique cultures before they feel the full impact of technological development.

Culture and Pattern

Culture refers to those ways of behaving that are learned and shared socially. As characteristic of all mankind, it is intimately related to the biological development of the species, for the ability of the brain to symbolize and the ability of other parts of the body to act in accord with the brain's messages made man capable of developing culture. But culture as displayed by any particular group is not a biological given; it includes all that knowledge and all those customs, attitudes, and beliefs that are learned by individuals from the members of the group in which they grow up. A culture is a particular way of life of a people. These "ways" cannot be seen directly, but they are expressed by behavior and, of course, by the product of some of that behavior, material things.

There are no generally agreed on units of culture, used by all anthropologists at all times in describing and comparing particular cultures. Traits, items, forms, complexes, elements, institutions—these are all words in use for relatively small units. For broader units there are such categories as language, technology, social organization, religion, and folklore, or the even broader and more objective division of culture into artifacts, sociofacts, and mentifacts—that is, articles made by man, social behavior, and ideas.

Nor have anthropologists agreed on any particular scheme for cutting up the globe into different cultures. They have, however, developed two different geographically-based ways of ordering their material. One is the concept of culture area and the other is the concept of community. A *culture area* is a geographical area occupied by groups having a number of significant culture traits in common—means of subsistence, social organization, and so on. Its boundaries are seldom clear-cut and depend on the weight given various cultural forms, on how many and which traits are picked as being typical. For example, the pre-Columbian North American Indians can be described as belonging to from three to thirteen culture areas, depending on what cultural elements are selected as significant. The extent of the area will also vary historically or shift completely—witness the futility today of thinking about North America according to any particular number of Indian culture areas.

Communities are small-scale samples of a culture. They may be bands, villages, rural communities, towns, or neighborhoods. People belonging to a particular ethnic or interest group and operating in a social system distinct from that of the rest of a heterogeneous urban neighborhood have also been called communities or partial communities. Any of these communities may have connections with other encompassing or complementary systems. Bands may—or may not—be parts of tribes, and villages and the like interconnect with other political and social systems. Ethnographies are actually community studies, although the tendency is to use the former name for studies of strange cultures and the latter for studies of more familiar ones.

Ethnography is so associated with the strange that for many its flavor is conveyed in the exotic sounds or unusual combinations of such words as *mana, tapu, totem, brideprice, couvade,* and *potlatch.* These words certainly attest to a wide variety of human behavior. Ethnographers have discovered, for example, that some peoples living on islands in the Pacific kept skulls or other relics of their ancestors in special places, or put odd-shaped rocks in their gardens, or fished with hooks made of an enemy's bones, because they believed great power—*mana*—to be associated with those objects. Other ethnographers described Polynesian chiefs who were thought to be so sacred that the very ground they walked on was dangerous and therefore forbidden—*tapu* or taboo—to commoners, and so the chiefs went forth on the shoulders of their retainers in order not to completely inconvenience their people. Or they described tribes in Australia that traced clan descent from and had symbolic relationship with some animal or plant or object—their *totem;* or Bantu tribes in Africa who gave livestock, cloth, and beer to their wives' families upon marriage, or upon the birth of the first child—the *brideprice.* Others wrote that when a baby was born among some South American jungle groups, the mother got up and went about her work while the father—in *couvade*—retired to his hammock and rested; or that in America on the Northwest Coast, an Indian's act of supreme vengeance was to destroy great quantities of his own property in the presence of his enemy—a special form of *potlatch.*

Some of these customs, and myriad others described, no longer prevail, but "peculiar" customs still pepper the globe. And if the histories of our own Western European civilization are ransacked for other illustrative tidbits (or perhaps if some of our present-day customs are looked at objectively), the odd ways of man seem virtually boundless. But the ways of man are not boundless, and they are not to be understood by any such itemization of strange behavior. Even the culture of any one particular group cannot be adequately described as a series of customs. A culture is not a list, but an overall pattern for living; and that pattern can be discovered only by seeing the relationship of each of the various cultural elements to the others. Any one part of a culture must be looked at in the context of the whole culture.

LOOKING FROM THE OUTSIDE

The anthropologist is an outsider. He tries to observe and describe an unfamiliar culture in as much detail as possible because it is by no means immediately clear how one item of behavior will connect with another, and what relationships will turn out to be the significant ones. His ideal goal is to give such a clear picture of the culture that one can predict from it how the culture's participants will act in any of the situations in which they are likely to find themselves as they go about their daily lives, from one year to the next. This is clearly an awesome order, and few anthropologists any longer go into the field without narrowing their goal to manageable proportions by selecting a focus of interest—social organization, leadership patterns, the effect of hunger on cultural forms, culture and personality, for just a few examples. Sometimes if enough is known about the particular culture, or similar ones, the field worker will go out armed with a hypothesis about the culture which he wants to test against the data. Even problem-oriented research, however, must cover as much of the whole culture as possible, partly because other anthropologists will want to use the data in other ways, but most importantly because culture is patterned and the particular relationship of its parts to each other and to the whole is not to be assumed but discovered through study.

The idea of "pattern" in general is of something laid out to be followed, and so *culture patterns* are, in a sense, plans for action, or "designs for living." They are the lifeways of any society, some of which are rigidly prescribed by the society and others of which are presented as permissible alternatives. The word *pattern* also refers to the effect or result of following a particular plan—"the work made in accordance to this design" is a dictionary definition—and it is this aspect that is emphasized when anthropologists describe the pattern of a culture as the way that the various elements of the culture are interconnected to form a working system. This way involves both the degree of interrelatedness of customs and the kinds of relationships exhibited.

In any society some cultural traits are more closely knit than others. These traits representing behavior and belief cluster around the performance of some activity, such as procuring and sharing food, bringing up children, providing for the inheritance of property, creating art, performing rites, and making war. All of these patterned activities can be divided and subdivided into a great variety of other systems, or grouped and regrouped with other patterned activities into a few wider patterns. For example, subsistence and settlement patterns are intimately related—nomadic pastoralists do not live in villages surrounded by fenced-off plots, and extensive horticulture is not practiced by people who travel about with tents. In a strange society, the anthropologist must have his mind alert to many less obvious connections; the distinctive associations that are made and those that are stressed in each culture form that culture's own unique pattern. The anthropologist must also be alert to the ways in which the real pattern of culture ("the work made") deviates from the ideal pattern ("the design"). He may discover the latter by consulting a few key informants as to the norms of behavior in the society, but he can discover the former only by observing actual behavior and how it varies from the prescribed patterns.

Cultures differ in the extent to which the patterning of any one activity overlaps or interlinks with that of others. The more technologically complex societies are characterized by a proliferation of different kinds of activities and groups, whereas in societies with simple technologies there is less differentiation and specialization; that is, each individual is apt to have much the same knowledge of the culture as has any other. A brief description of the culture of the Siriono Indians of eastern Bolivia illustrates the interconnectedness of one behavior pattern—the dietary—with others in a relatively homogeneous society. Allan Holmberg, the anthropologist who studied this group, was interested in the effect of hunger on cultural forms, and he sought out "a group of perennially hungry human beings" for his field work.[2]

Small, seminomadic bands of Siriono eked out a precarious existence in the Bolivian tropical forest as hunters and food-gatherers, supplementing their food supply by some gardening. Hunting with bow and arrow, or occasionally with a randomly picked-up club, was by far the most important activity of the men. Alone or in small groups, they followed the numerous trails out of camp before daybreak, to search the forest—particularly near water holes—for monkey, wild pig, deer, tapir, alligator, and other game animals and fowl of the area. Hunting was hard, long, tiring work, and many times the hunters returned empty-handed in spite of their cleverness in stalking and in imitating animal noises. Monkey of various sorts was the most common catch. Tapir, the prize catch because of its size, was rarely brought in because, being nocturnal, it fed while the hunters slept and slept while they stalked—only occasionally betraying itself by its sleeping wheeze. The few kinds of fish caught were taken with bow and arrow, too, from overhanging trees, because while the Siriono knew about fishhooks, they did not have boats or rafts to take them out into deep water. Other fish were clubbed and scooped up during the dry season where dying ponds trapped them.

Food-gathering was second only to hunting in importance. Gathering was a family affair. Men, women, and children collected palm cabbage, fruits, and wild honey—the honey being used for both food and fermented drink. During the wet season when the ground became swampy, the Siriono sought out higher sites where palm and wild fruit trees grew, and where they cleared and planted small plots near their huts or near favorite waterside hunting spots. These gardens, too, were family products. After the tedious work of clearing only a small patch, maize, manioc, and a few other things might be planted, using only a simple digging stick, then tended sporadically, and finally harvested.

Sharing the game brought in from the hunt was customary, but it occasioned a great deal of discussion and quarreling. Usually there was only enough to share with one's family. Certain animals, including tapir, were not supposed to be eaten by the hunter himself lest his luck in hunting them in the future fail him. In these cases, exchanges of food would be made with another family, and in other cases extra food might be given away in the expectation of future reciprocity—an expectation that usually had to be pressed for fulfillment. Prestige among the Siriono was closely associated with food. Not only were the best hunters the most highly regarded, but among the women the good food collectors were selected for marriage with little regard to other skills, and food was a lure in extramarital relations.

Food was cooked simply, either roasted whole or in pieces, or in clay pots set directly on the fire. In the single hut that the band occupied each family had its own fire, built on the ground next to a hammock. Women did most of the cooking when in camp, but children early learned how to cook, and men often roasted meat. They knew no way of preserving or storing food, so it was eaten right away; besides, delay in partaking might mean that someone else would get to it first. A main meal was usually taken at the end of the day, but eating went on at any hour, often at night or in secret to avoid others asking for some. For the same reason, apparently, no etiquette was observed in eating; food was bolted while eyes were kept downcast. The people expressed little preference in foods, appreciating all kinds.

The few ceremonies practiced by the Siriono involved food. Food was presented in marriage, and certain foods were taboo for girls at puberty, for women during pregnancy, and for both the mother and the father in connection with birth. There were also food taboos for the hunter, which were magical ways of assuring the success of the hunt. There was no magic connected with the planting of the gardens, but Moon, the mythical hero, was supposed to have given the bands most of the plants.

Food occupied the waking and sleeping thoughts of the Siriono. It figured prominently in their dreams, and begging for shares and quarreling about distribution seemed to form the bulk of their conversation. This anxiety about food, the anthropologist thought, was also displayed by the Siriono's claiming to be hungry even after having eaten quite heartily.

Thus the dietary pattern—the actual procuring, sharing, preparing, and eating of food—can be traced in its close connections with the simple technology of the Siriono (the bow and arrow, the digging stick, the clay pots, and their use), their social interaction and organization (the division of labor between the men and the women, marriage, the family gardens, family cooking and sleeping space in the communal hut, leadership, exchange relationships with other families), and their ideas about the supernatural (ceremonies, magic, taboos, the Moon myth). So can the particular patterned activities of any society be traced throughout the culture, demonstrating the direct and indirect connections that tie the whole together either loosely or, as with the Siriono, tightly.

Pattern also implies, besides these connections, some extent of internal consistency in the traits and patterns making up the whole. That is, the relationship between the different parts must be characterized by a certain fit. The fit may be one of agreement on the basic values and goals in life or it may be one of balance, where one element complements another.

The positive values of a culture are those goals and ways of behaving that the society deems most desirable, and the negative are those disliked. On one level these are attitudes and judgments about right and wrong that are made explicit by both word and deed, but on a deeper level they are the unstated principles that underlie the overt behavior. Anthropologists describe these basic, implicit values in various ways—as the ethos, or configuration, or theme, or plot, or even obsession of the culture. But however the notion is elaborated, the whole network of patterned behavior is seen as linked to the underlying value system, and this is seen as giving the culture much of its unique quality. The potlatch can serve as an example. As practiced by a number of American Indian groups living on the Northwest Coast from Puget Sound to Alaska, it was a ceremony by which a man divested himself of quantities of his accumulated wealth either by publicly presenting it to invited guests or by publicly destroying it.[3] The giver of the potlatch gained prestige according to the amount of property distributed or destroyed, and the recipients were shamed until they were able to reciprocate, with interest.

This one ceremony had ramifications throughout the culture. First, there were a number of reasons and occasions for giving potlatches. They were given to celebrate marriage and the building of a house and at the name-changing ceremonies held to advance the social status of one's children and to enhance one's own prestige, and were accompanied by lavish boasting. Chieftainship was involved, since potlatches were given not only to maintain the reputation of a chief's household, but most importantly to validate an heir's claim to the succession. Other potlatches were given to avenge oneself against rivals, or to wipe out an insult or humiliation of some kind. The peak of glory and a sure way to defame a rival was the destruction of all of one's property, but—not unexpectedly—this was not a popular potlatch to give. Besides the actual exchange and competitive distribution of the property, the pattern of the potlatch is exhibited in the ways the property—usually blankets, copper plaques, and shell money, but sometimes slaves, canoes, or whole houses—was accumulated. The accumulation of blankets was particularly important and involved an elaborate system of high interest on blankets loaned. The potlatch touched religious life in the association of certain religious ceremonial societies with some of the potlatches, and recreational life in the giving of parody potlatches, the comic tearing to pieces of a last remaining blanket on some occasions, and the repeated telling of stories about famous potlatches. The potlatching pattern involved so much of the total culture, usually in such a consistent way, that some anthropologists have felt justified in describing the values that it so vividly expresses as basic to the whole pattern of the culture. They see pride, great concern for social rank, and liberality matched with aggressiveness as dominant tribal attitudes, coloring the entire way of life of these groups.

The proposition that cultures are integrated wholes, with each part consistent with the other parts and with underlying values, has proven very helpful in understanding them. Nevertheless, the idea should be used with caution. First, consistency—that is, integration of a culture in accord with a system of basic values—is a tendency and not a perfect accomplishment in cultures. Any one culture, even a very homogeneous one, has traits exhibiting conflicting values. E. Adamson Hoebel, a student of the Cheyenne, points out that among the Indians of our Great Plains there was a cluster of traits—among them vision-seeking through self-denial and torture in order to acquire power and glory, bravery in battle, and boastfulness—emphasizing the model of the aggressive, individualistic "egotistical warrior." At the same time, however, another group of traits existed that stressed the self-restraint, gentleness, and generosity of the "considerate peace chief."[4] A strain of consistency, as it has been called, is present in all cultures, but it is a strain that anthropologists first look for in a society's institutions and the behavior of individuals, and then describe; they do not assume it or insist upon finding it always manifested.

Second, and in further elaboration of the first caution, a great deal must be known about how a particular society works before jumping to conclusions about either the degree or kind of cultural integration achieved. Holmberg has suggested, as a conclusion of his study of the Siriono, that their lifelong struggle to get enough to eat, and the accompanying anxiety, is part of a pattern of apathy manifest in relationships with one another. He cites their habit of deserting the aged and the sick, who not only cannot keep up with the band in its travels, but also consume food without contributing any—the ultimate offense. Holmberg tells a story about the Indian, Ekwataia, to illustrate how ingrained a Siriono's lack of concern for his fellows was. Ekwataia, a crippled bachelor, lost his way one dark night returning from hunting. Just a few hundred yards from camp he called for help, either for fire or for answering cries to guide him back to camp. No one paid any attention and he finally gave up, at which point his sister in camp remarked that a jaguar had probably gotten him. Ekwataia spent the night in a tree to save himself from jaguars and returned the following morning with his catch. His sister's main reaction was to lament the small size of her portion.

From this description, one might assume that in other societies in which the struggle for existence is arduous the aged and the sick are also deserted and apathy is shown toward the dire straits of others. Indeed, similar examples have been given for the Eskimo. But the same kind of consistency is not apparent in another South American group, the Kaingang of Brazil, studied by Jules Henry.[5] The Kaingang were "hunger-ridden" nomadic hunters, too, similar to the Siriono in many ways. Their obsession was not so much food as feuds, however; their psychological adjustment to life did not follow the Siriono model. The Kaingang are described as fearful, boastful, ferocious, and suicidally aggressive. Far from being apathetic, they were warmly affectionate with their own relatives and friends. They did not desert their own people who were too old or feeble to fend for themselves, but carried them on their backs along the way. Henry states that even when Kaingang were wounded in battle or surrounded by an enemy, "the accusation 'you are deserting me' would always bring back the fleeing Indian, even to his own death." Thus, the pattern of values of any one culture can be discerned only through intimate knowledge of that culture.

There are, however, varying portrayals of the same culture, each based on intimate knowledge, and this is only partly because workers have gone to the field with different focusses of interest around which they gathered their data. All anthropologists, for instance, do not agree that the values exemplified by the potlatch ceremony are indeed so thoroughly integrating of Northwest Coast culture as has been indicated. Anthropologists also debate the core values, interrelationships, and internal consistency of other cultures; there is probably some measure of disagreement on these points wherever more than one anthropologist has studied the same group. (Documentation abounds, often limned in acid, in the communications and book review sections of the professional journals.) Disagreement is probably inherent in a situation where the process of investigating partakes of what is being investigated—human behavior; however, it is also valuable in that through such controversy different aspects of a culture are brought forth and examined.[6] Insights must be various to aid comprehension of the many-sided phenomenon of culture. Anthropologists, as outsiders looking in at a culture and attempting to interpret it, are each bound to have somewhat different views. It is to the credit of both their scientific training and their humanistic outlook that they have accumulated a body of knowledge that purports to see other cultures from the inside. That is, they have realized the necessity of making special efforts to see a way of life from the viewpoint of the participants themselves before analyzing that way in terms of patterns perceived from the outside.

LOOKING FROM THE INSIDE

The Siriono hunter in his hammock is prey to conflicting emotions. He knows that he must find food because he and his family are hungry, because his prestige depends on being known as a good hunter, and perhaps because he has his eye on a woman who will respond only if he comes to her with morsels of wild pig meat. On the other hand, the hunt is long and tiring. If he goes, jungle thorns will tear at him, insects will feast on him, and worst of all, if he returns with no catch, not only will the day-long food quest have been pointless, but he will also be mocked for his failure. Perhaps there is already food in camp and he can beg some—if he goes hunting all day he certainly won't get his share of what there is. With these thoughts the Siriono hunter is likely to lie there in his hammock "until the hunger drive, or the social pressure to go hunting, becomes unbearable."

This description is one of the few places in Holmberg's monograph where the reader has a feeling of being "inside" Siriono culture, of really understanding how a Siriono might look out on his hard life. One might, perhaps, identify with Ekwataia crouching in the dark in his tree; we are hardly "inside" his silent sister who was willing to leave him to his fate, although we may account environmentally for her callous behavior. But it is precisely the sister who catches our imagination. We want to understand how she, and those other Siriono who shared her apathy, viewed a world in which such behavior was so customary as to cause no comment.

Attempts to view cultures from the inside are exercises in translation, and the exercises represent different methodologies. Even though he is an outsider, the anthropologist who lives intimately with the community he is studying and who describes a culture as a whole, or relates one part of it to its other parts, has already taken long strides away from his own cultural vantage toward his subject's. The following steps are more important than the theoretically possible final step—that is, the complete assumption of another culture's point of view—because our interest is in understanding the culture and not in becoming a full-fledged participant in it.

These exercises in cultural translation are sometimes contained in studies of culture and personality, where culture patterns are related to personality patterns; or in attempts to obtain the world view of the culture-bearer, that is, to understand his basic philosophical orientations; or in efforts to describe the total environment and experience of the culture-bearer in terms of his own definitions and categories only—the so-called new ethnography. Two approaches are vital to all of these attempts: one, humanistic and empathetic, and the other, scientific and systematic. They are variously commingled in the work of anthropologists seeking to describe a culture from the inside. In some works insights about the emotions that accompany specific be-havior—the "yearning, hope, or fear," as Jules Henry has said—are important elements toward understanding; and in others highly technical linguistic analyses are employed. These two emphases, and the great range of possible emphases between them, have the same aim, which is to discover how members of the society charac-teristically view their world, how they think and feel about it. The interest is still in the patterning of culture, but the stress is on how the Eskimo, or the Siriono, or the participant in whatever culture sees the patterns, not on how the anthropologist may analyze them. The job starts with the individual, and it makes a difference which indi-vidual's outlook is being investigated, what position he occupies in the society, and whether he is of a philosophic or prosaic turn of mind. Nevertheless, any individual in a culture is, by and large, typ-ical. He is typical, first, in the way that he classifies his experience and his environment; second, in what facets of his experience and environment interest him the most; and third, in how he sees his own relationships to the different parts of his world. Each of these factors can be explored.

Attempts to understand how people classify their experience, what categories they recognize, must begin with finding out what names they give to things and continue with observing what behavior and beliefs are associated with the names. For a minor but helpfully concrete example, some groups use only one name for what we call orange and yellow, or for what we call blue and green, or two names for what we call only black. Tests have shown that in spite of this way of naming things these people can distinguish blue from green as well as we can. They see blue and they see green, but culturally they don't care to comment on the difference. That is, they see colors as we see them, but they group and separate what they see in a different way, a culturally determined way. Also, we, too, can distinguish the two blacks if we want to, and we can group and separate colors dif-ferently according to specialized interests, as in the marketing of commodities where color is a significant attribute—paint, lipstick, clothing, and so on are almost interminably classified, subclassified and reclassified according to hue.

The vocabulary of any language reflects the experience and interests of the language users. The stock anthropological example of this, first offered by Franz Boas, is the words in the Eskimo language for snow: one for snow on the ground, another for falling snow, another for drifting snow, and still another for an existing snowdrift, but none for the general idea of snow. In our culture, we perceive the differences in these "snow" phenomena, and can easily express them by using the root word *snow*, but our experience and our interests have not led us to separate them by distinct names. An almost equally classic example is the *yam* vocabulary of the Trobriand Islanders of New Guinea, whose subsistence leaned heavily on their yam crops and to whom yams had social and ritual significance. A big yam had one name, an overripe one another, one with shoots another, and so on, through hundreds of names for the two botanical varieties that were grown. Again, the aggressive, fear-ridden, feuding Kaingang had a large vocabulary to express the idea "kill."

Anthropologists have long had greatest success in discovering a culture's categories in the area of kinship. They long ago disciplined themselves to keep their own culturally learned ideas about family relationships in the background while they worked at discovering how, in a particular culture, an individual (called *ego* in kinship analyses) classified people—that is, how he grouped them in relationship to himself. Biological relationships are the same everywhere, of course, but societies the world over have elaborated a great many different ways of grouping and treating blood, in-law, and simulated relatives. For example, ego's view of those related to him genealogically may include all of his mother's sisters as mothers and their children as brothers and sisters, thus overriding the fact of biological distance of relationship; or it may consider father's sisters and father's sisters' daughters as in the same category, thus ignoring the difference of generation; or it may group all children of parents' siblings together as cousins, thus overlooking the difference of sex; and so on throughout a number of possible combinations based on a series of criteria for classification.

Patterns of kinship terminology and behavior more nearly approximate an inside view when the emotional cast of the relationships is explored and when it is discovered how individuals actually use the ideal system. For example, the Kaingang are described as having a kinship system which requires that a man at marriage give up loyalties derived from common descent or residence in favor of loyalty to his wife's kin, with all of the reciprocal obligations that are entailed. Because of plural marriages and intermarriages within the band, the resulting ties of kinship are theoretically very complex. Henry asserts, however, that actually "the Kaingang go through life supremely indifferent" to the putative system, picking for themselves which in-laws (who are probably also genealogically related) they wish for allies, and disregarding the others. Henry recounts: "With indignation in his voice my best informant denied that his wife's brothers and sisters were his in-laws. What, call those people in-laws, who never gave him anything? He should say not. At first they were too young to give him anything, and even now that they were grown up they ignored him."[7] James West, a pseudonymous anthropologist who worked in Plainville, a pseudonymous American farming community, describes a similar situation.[8] The ideal behavior toward kin taught in Plainville at the time the study was made was cooperation in work and exchange of products between closely related families, headed by fathers, their sons, and brothers—a system that had worked well in frontier days when these families lived close together and depended on one another. Actually, however, these extended family ties had lost much of their former meaning because of migration and changes in economic patterns, and even where these ties were observed they were apt to be regarded as burdensome.

Other examples of behavior patterns in more intimate perspective, that is, from an inside point of view, are contained in ethnographical descriptions of polygynous households, where evidence of affection and jealousy, favoritism and cooperation gives the flavor of reality to that marriage practice, or in descriptions of families that reckon descent and inheritance through the mother's line and hence to the sister's son, but where behavior nonetheless attests to paternal warmth.

The pervasiveness of our own culture's terms of reference have made other areas of life more difficult to classify according to an inner view. The custom of the brideprice serves as a first example. In our society the distribution of goods belongs to a category that we do not hesitate to label *economic*, and the word *price* to us normally means the cost of buying whatever it is that is being distributed. In many societies around the world substantial accumulations of wealth are turned over to a new wife's family by the husband, and this was initially called a brideprice. Anthropologists soon pointed out, however, that the bride has in no sense been on the market, that no commercial transaction has taken place. From the point of view of the individual practicing the custom, the wealth changing hands may have been to indemnify the girl's family for her loss, or to establish her obligations to him. It is part of a whole pattern of reciprocal obligations, not only between the marriage partners but also between their families. Although wealth has changed hands, it is fully as much of a social as it is an economic transaction. Consequently most anthropologists no longer speak of the *brideprice,* but use the term *bridewealth* in an effort to more nearly approximate the point of view of the culture.

For another example, the division of labor is a concept developed in our society to apply to the specialization of work. It is primarily an economic idea, although of course the specialized work is done by social groups. When we apply the idea to another culture, again there is a problem of translation. Division of labor by sex is the most common kind of specialization, and the ethnographies are full of such descriptions as "the women cook, make clothes, care for the children, and the men hunt and carry on wars." These descriptions are helpful in seeing the pattern of culture—from the outside. In looking from the inside, however, we find that in many societies this kind of description will not do; it neglects the use of magic as a means to accomplish an end. Magic, which may be defined as a technique for manipulating the supernatural in order to achieve a desired result and which is manifested in observances, incantations, rituals, or taboos, must be taken into account in outlining the division of labor, by sex or otherwise. An old Eskimo once told an ethnographer, "It is a mistake to think that women are weaker than men in hunting pursuits. The home incantations are stronger than those pronounced in the wilderness. In vain man walks around, searching; but those that sit by the lamp are really strong for they know how to call the game to the shore!" Bronislaw Malinowski, famous for his intensive fieldwork among the Trobriand Islanders, has described how closely magic was bound to technical means in some activities in that society.[10] For example, garden magic was regarded as a regular part of the tending of the public gardens. Each technological step—clearing the ground, tilling, weeding, harvesting—had a corresponding magical one, with its specially designated place in the whole gardening process. There was also a general magic for growth applied to the activity as a whole.

These examples do not mean that the Eskimo or the Trobriand Islanders did not see a difference between practical technology and magic ritual as ways of working toward an end. Probably all societies have recognized a distinction between the natural and the supernatural (although one anthropologist, at least, has doubted it). Malinowski wrote that "magic and practical work are, in native ideas, inseparable from each other, though they are not confused." The Trobriand Islanders knew what had to be done by hard labor; they knew that magic would not make plants grow in barren soil. But they also realized that no amount of industry alone could successfully guard against pests, blights, bush pigs, drought, or other happenstances that might prevent a garden from flourishing. This point of view permeated the whole culture. Magic was used also in connection with overseas sailing expeditions, to ensure success in warfare or good health, or to make one beautiful and loved, and so on. From a Trobriander's vantage, no consideration of the division of the work to be done could ignore the magical.

This version of division of labor, incidentally, sheds light on the puzzling, widely-distributed custom of couvade, by which the father participates in the birth rites, either taking the mother's place in bed or, as among the Siriono, merely observing the same taboos and rites as does the mother. These practices partake of the magical and seem to be directed toward a safe birth and the subsequent welfare of the child and parents. The father who observed the couvade to ensure an easy delivery and a normal child may be compared to the Eskimo woman who recited incantations to ensure her man a good hunt.

The concern for achieving an inside view of kinship, marriage customs, division of labor and magic, and any other practice is a traditional one in anthropology. It finds a more systematic and rigorous expression, however, in some of the methods of the "new ethnography," which set up procedures to guard against the ethnographer's approaching his subject with his own categories—western scientific or traditional—in mind. Ideally, the new ethnographer elicits the categories of the culture bit by bit by sets of questions carefully structured, first, to link a word or other linguistic form with an objectively designated unit from the total environment, and second, to establish the relationships—inclusive or contrastive—between the various units so named. If the units are plants, the ethnographer who follows this procedure will discover how the culture-bearer names and groups plants, and how he uses them and feels about them. He will have an insider's view of the flora—an ethnobotany—not a list of those plants from the Linnaean classification that are present in the area. The recommended procedure is so exacting and time-consuming that no new ethnography exists, only small pieces of it for scattered cultures.

Harold Conklin provided an example of ethnobotany in a study of the system of agriculture practiced by the Hanunóo, a small society living inland on Mindoro Island in the Philippines.[11] Their natural environment included a remarkably complex plant life that numbered well over a thousand different species. The Hanunóo were well aware of this complexity. In fact, they were so knowledgeable about the flora and so interested in it culturally—using plants intensively for food and medicine and in their ritual and technology—that their own plant categories numbered several hundred more than the species recognized by botanists. On the most general level, the Hanunóo divided plant life into three groups, according to whether stem growth was grassy, woody, or vine-like. On the most specific level, criteria such as leaf shape, color, size, taste, smell, and habitat were used. The Hanunóo also differentiated plants on the basis of whether they were cultivated or wild, or protected wild plants, such as fruit trees. Further, types of vegetation—that is, plants growing in association—were classified into six major and many minor types. The latter were those growing in certain environments, and included coastal, streamside, cliff, and houseyard vegetation, and even plant associations growing on old house sites or in stump holes. The major associations directly reflected the Hanunóo system of shifting agriculture, and described the vegetation in fields newly cultivated, cultivated crops plus secondary growth, areas in various stages of fallowing, and primary forests and grassy areas perhaps never before cleared.

A second important step in interpreting cultures, after delimiting categories, is the attempt to find out what facets of a group's environment and experience interest it the most; in other words, to discover what the culture stresses, in accordance with what principles. The naming of things by itself, of course, involves stress on what the culture considers worthy of comment. But there is, beyond this, the question of what is considered to be particularly important, what features dominate the view of the world held by people in a particular culture. Considered from the outside, this is in great part the the value system of a culture, those ideas and attitudes that are expressed again and again by various customs and institutions, as the potlatch and other customs express the importance of social rank among the Indians of the Northwest Coast. For an inside view, the reach is for a deeper understanding of the philosophy underlying the cultural values and of the individual's basic conception of the nature of things. Two attempts by anthropologists to arrive at the characteristic world view of a culture, one of the Kota of India and the other of the Tzotzil of Mexico, illustrate this kind of an attempt to understand a culture.

The Kota are traditional craftsmen living in villages scattered among those of three other groups on the Nilgiri Plateau of southern India. David Mandelbaum, the anthropologist who studied their way of life, tried to understand how the Kota regarded the world about them by analyzing the quarrels that frequently accompanied a particular funeral rite.[12] At the final funeral observances which marked the end of mourning held at the end of the ceremonial year, a ritual of bowing occurred that expressed respectful farewell to the deceased by his kinsmen, and also established their status as kinsmen in good standing. Quarrels took place when Kota men belonging to a conservative village faction tried to prevent men from bowing who belonged to a reform group, membership in which was symbolized by short haircuts. The intimation was that these men were not true Kota. This was a recurring situation and was an uppermost concern of the Kota during the anthropologist's stay. He traced it to a Kota world view that stressed man's relationship to other men. The Kota accepted both the natural and the supernatural spheres of life very matter-of-factly. They were not greatly interested in nature or in material things, and while they considered their gods powerful, they also thought that by the proper rituals they could be successfully manipulated. Nature and the gods alike had to be dealt with, but neither was considered any great problem. One's fellow man was a different matter; he constituted a real threat. The Kota felt that they must constantly struggle with other men to defend their individual rights and their social position. This is evident in much of the material collected by Mandelbaum and is illustrated by the contention surrounding the bowing. The reform Kota felt that their rights were in jeopardy, that if they were prevented from bowing it reflected on them as kinsmen and Kota. The ideal Kota, it was thought, "must react sharply to any possible slight, instantly jealous of his status." Anger and common sense were considered the most desirable personal attributes, anger so that a man could defend his rights vigorously, common sense so that he could know when those rights were endangered.

Another anthropologist, Calixta Guiteras Holmes, used a different approach to the same problem.[13] Working with a general knowledge of the culture, she attempted to understand the world view of the Tzotzil Indians of the Chiapas highlands in Mexico by interviewing intensively one Tzotzil man over a long period of time. The Tzotzil, it developed, focussed their interest on the supernatural. They conceived of the whole cosmos as being, like home and field, in the shape of a square, and as being animate. All nature was thought to be permeated by ruling powers, the source of all thought and of good and evil. The good powers either worked for, or by prayer or magic could be made to achieve, the well-being and preservation of man and of his lesser gods, the sun and the moon. But other powers were malevolent and bent on man's annihilation. To keep one's very soul safe from them it was necessary to take a great number of culturally prescribed precautions. Good was associated with light and evil with dark; the Tzotzil informant told the anthropologist, "In the cultivated fields there is neither shadow nor darkness, it is open land and we are not afraid; in the forest it is dark and there are snakes, sink holes, caves, [and evil apparitions] . . ., and we are afraid." The evil spirits were thought to be working to destroy man during the night, and so as soon as day was done the villagers closed themselves tightly in their houses. The earth was the most powerful force, giving and taking life. In Guiteras Holmes' words, "She brings forth and fosters all creatures, but is simultaneously their common grave. She relentlessly swallows back, as a monster, the beings that she produces. All that live on her surface come from her interior and return there. She is all-producing, all-maintaining, all-devouring." Man was thought to have two souls, one eternal and the other an animal soul, apt to be destructive, that resided in a forest creature and by which each man was associated with threatening nature throughout his life.

Unlike the Kota outlook, with its casual acceptance of nature and almost mechanical manipulation of the supernatural, the Tzotzil world view focussed on a powerful nature in league with fearsome supernatural forces with which man had constantly to deal and against which man had always to be on guard. The culture of the Kota stressed the relationship of man with man, that of the Tzotzil stressed man's relationship with the supernatural, which by definition resided in all nature.

The underlying philosophy of a culture involves not only what is stressed in that culture but also how the individual defines his relationship to all that he confronts. Different peoples have very distinct ways of thinking and feeling about nature. Some groups, like the Kota, see such natural objects as trees and stones simply as things, while others personalize these objects. The Kaingang, like the Tzotzil, associated nature with the supernatural. They were deeply fearful of supernatural beings, and they were also violently enraged at them and the threat that they represented. Once, when an epidemic struck, a Kaingang frantically beat the air and the trees, threatening the supernatural beings that he held responsible: "I'll kill you....I'll kill you." Similarly, a Kaingang would scowl and growl at the thunder to threaten the storm away, or when it came, fearfully entreat it to depart. Jules Henry points out that the Kaingang made the same emotional appeal to the elements that they made to people.

Some groups feel dominated by nature, at its arbitrary and violent disposal; others feel that nature is to be subjugated or controlled; and

still others think of themselves as continuous with nature, a harmoni-
ous part of it, and their values center on seeking to understand and
perpetuate this close relationship. For an example, the upper-middle-
class professional people living in Crestwood Heights, a pseudonymous suburban community in central Canada that was studied by a
team of sociologists, felt that power was on their side in the man-
nature equation, that they were—or should be—masters of their fate
in regard to both nature and the supernatural.[14] This is in strong contrast to the intimate relationship with nature of the Wintu Indians
of California, as described by Dorothy Lee. She quotes an old man,
no longer able to provide for himself as praying:

> I cannot go up to the mountains in the west to you, deer;
> I cannot kill you and bring you home. . .
> You, water, I can never dip you up and fetch you home again. . . .
> You who are wood, you wood, I cannot carry you home on my shoulder.[15]

Lee comments that "this is not the speech of one who has plucked the
fruits of nature by brute force; it is the speech of a friend."

Anthropologists have also described how people in different cultures conceive of themselves in relation to the rest of mankind, time,
space, or the whole cosmos. In Crestwood Heights, people felt themselves in control of their environment, and they lived in the present
while planning for the near-future, with almost no thought for the
past. The Yir Yoront of Australia, a technologically simple hunting
and gathering folk studied by Lauriston Sharp, viewed the world
much differently.[16] For them, time was divided into two parts. First,
there was a distant, mythical period during which larger-than-life
ancestral beings established the clans and their associated totems,
which represented in detail the whole world of the Yir Yoront. This
period was succeeded by a new order, in which life was unchanging,
an eternal mirroring of the past. For the Yir Yoront, before contact
with European culture forced a new view, past, present, and future
were one.

In all of the efforts to discover how members of diverse cultures
categorize, stress, and relate to their environment and experience,
language plays a very special role because, of course, it is the method
by which the categories, interests, and relationships of a culture are
most obviously expressed. Anthropologists must work through the
languages of the groups they study in their attempts to arrive at an
inside view of the cultures. That is, they make discoveries about the
language, and then see if and how these correlate with the culture.
The Eskimo snow vocabulary and the Trobriand yam vocabulary are
examples of the correlation between the vocabulary of a language and

the interests of a culture, and this type of language-culture correlation is common. Ethnographers expect a people's vocabulary to give clues to important aspects of their culture. Indeed, when trying to discover culturally recognized categories, they start by finding out how a culture-bearer names things, sometimes analyzing a linguistic form by searching for changed meaning as each of its components is changed.

Other language-culture correlations are sought which would link linguistic structure with patterns of seeing (perception) and patterns of thinking (cognition). In these attempts, grammar is considered a possible clue to the underlying philosophy or world view of a people. It has been suggested, for example, that the Navaho view of nature as composed of personal forces is evident in the way that they would say "hunger (or thirst, or water) is killing me" instead of "I am hungry (or thirsty, or drowning)."[17] Another example from the Navaho is the stress on verbs in their language and on action in their culture, as contrasted with the stress in our language on nouns and in our culture on things. Navaho verbs vary in form according to conditions ignored in other languages—whether the acting subject is round or long and narrow, scratchy or smooth, and so on, and whether the action is accomplished by one means or another and other subtleties of action such as direction and distance. Most attempts to link definitively linguistic structure with a basic culture pattern lean heavily on the linguistic evidence itself, the reasoning being that these people say things this way, therefore they probably think this way. Studies that present non-linguistic verification by anthropologists thoroughly conversant with the culture they are reporting are considered by some as validly convincing and by others as more intuitional than scientific.

Some linguistic anthropologists have gone further than stating that language reflects modes of thought and have suggested that language molds or constrains perception and cognition. According to this idea, it is not simply that we only say what we know and feel, but that what we know and feel is shaped by what we habitually say. There is little doubt that vocabulary, by calling attention to certain parts of the environment and of a group's experience, ensures that these parts are perceived and thought about in a particular way, and it is quite probable that other aspects of language act similarly. In its extreme form, this idea or hypothesis is that language directs perception and cognition to such an extent that it actually determines the underlying values or themes of a culture. The evidence does not seem to support such a supremely causal role for language. Language itself changes and is affected by other aspects of the culture. And in spite of the important role of language in culture, there are other ways of indicating inner experience; that is, communication is nonverbal as well as verbal. The connection between language and culture is very close and intricately knit, but it is one in which the language, the rest of the culture, and an individual's thoughts and feelings affect one another reciprocally. The problem becomes, in any particular case among the diverse cultures of the world, how and the extent to which each of these elements affects the others.

From the substitution of the word *bridewealth* for *brideprice* to a rigorous semantic analysis of a linguistic form is a long methodological journey, and anthropologists differ on which of the steps along the way will prove most fruitful. However, the aim of describing a culture from the inside is ambitious, and can only benefit, in the long run, from multiple approaches. The goal, ultimately, is to again look at the cultures studied from the outside, objectively and comparatively, but armed with a fuller understanding of the unique qualities of each.

Social Structure and Function

Culture is completely dependent on and cannot exist without people living together in groups over time—in other words, without society. Society and culture are different aspects of the same thing: people living together and behaving in a certain way; and both must be investigated in the same way, by observing life in actual communities. The two ideas cannot be separated, but they can be distinguished, and most but not all anthropologists find it useful to do so. People cannot live together in communities without behaving in certain ways (that is, all societies have culture), and people cannot behave in certain ways without living together (all cultures belong to societies). But if one wants to arrive at an understanding of how cultures develop and how societies work, the distinction of *culture,* as learned patterns of action, from *society,* as the interacting people having those patterns, is helpful. The two words are frequently used interchangeably with no violence to their meaning, as in "in this society..." or "in this culture..." such-and-such is done. The distinction is emphasized here because it is relevant to a discussion of social structure.

Social relationships, made up of regularly repeated kinds of interaction between people, are patterned by culture. They are, as was remarked about language, part of culture yet peculiarly important to it. Most cultural data are derived by observing social interaction, and this interaction is the basis of both cultural continuity and culture change. That is, while culture molds social behavior, social behavior also transforms culture. Analyzing these processes depends on understanding the cultural and social aspects of human behavior. In making general statements about human behavior, however, careful anthropologists repeat over and over "society and culture" or speak of "sociocultural" phenomena, thus putting together for synthesis what they have separated for analysis.

A perplexing question of names for things is involved in understanding social and cultural data. One of the difficulties besetting social scientists is the precise definition of words that are professionally current, but which have been adopted from everyday usage. Terms starting out with common sense definitions soon acquire more exact ones. However, sometimes several scientists sharpen the same words in somewhat diverging ways, and it is only with time—if ever—that rapprochement takes place. In the meantime, the literature is filled with explanations of what authors mean by certain words, or what they think others mean by them, and of how these words compare with still others that are being used in a similar sense. Naturally, this makes for a certain amount of confusion to the detriment of scholarly communication. Even—or perhaps especially—such a centrally important concept as culture is subject to a variety of interpretations.[18] *Society*, too, has different meanings. Sometimes the word is used to mean the form taken by the social relations of the people making up a group or community instead of the people themselves. More often, however, this particular aspect of society is expressed by other terms, including *social structure*, which is the one used here. It is not too important a point because all society has form or structure, just as all culture has form or pattern. Using these terms for form is only calling particular attention to what is inherent in the concepts of society and culture.

Pattern, structure, system, organization, even *institution,* are all words for much the same kind of phenomenon, and are often used interchangeably, or one is used in definition of another. They all refer to some kind of a whole, "an orderly working totality" with interrelated parts. Each whole is composed of its constituent parts and their connecting and dependent relationships. In turn, these wholes are not isolates, but may themselves be considered as parts of a larger entity. And the wholes are not exclusive; entities overlap or intersect other entities; different wholes may be of interest at different times for different reasons. The "totality" is considered as one only in certain contexts.

The word *system* is almost generic for this kind of phenomenon. In biology we are used to thinking of the respiratory system and the vascular system, for example, working within the larger whole of the human body. In the social sciences we speak of the political system, the technological system, and the economic, or ideological, or social system in much the same way, as operating, with interconnections, within the larger society. The word *institution* is similarly used, although usually for smaller-scale phenomena. Sometimes it refers to sprawling systems, such as religion or government, oftener to complexes of custom, such as marriage, family, or couvade, and at still other times to specific organizations, such as church, school, and special interest groups.

As has been indicated, anthropologists most commonly use the word *pattern* when the whole-with-interrelated-parts that is being considered is a culture or a part of a culture that can in turn be considered as an entity, such as particular activities or other closely knit clusters of cultural elements. The social structure of a particular group of people is the way they subgroup and regroup themselves, the way they sort themselves out by age, sex, class, interests, or various other criteria, to get things done. This way is culturally patterned; in other words, how an individual should behave toward other individuals and groups in his society is learned along with and in relation to the other expectations of his culture. It is, however, a particularly important pattern of culture, basic to and interweaving with all other patterns; that is, all activities, including economic, political, and religious ones are socially organized. Because of this, many anthropologists prefer to approach the way people are organized from the point of view of society rather than of culture, and they speak of it often not as "a pattern of culture" but as "the structure of society"—or "social structure." This is purely—one is tempted to say insignificantly—a matter of analytical concept: the facts being analyzed are facts of human social behavior whether the analysis is primarily in terms of "culture pattern" or "social structure."

By *social structure*, then, most anthropologists mean the way the people in a society customarily group themselves and interact with each other, how the society is made up. *Social system* and *social organization* are used synonymously, although not perhaps so fashionably. There are variations in usage, however. For example, *system* is sometimes used for the sociocultural whole, with structural and other cultural aspects, as well as how these function in the society, considered as subsumed parts of it. Or, conversely, the whole structure of a society is said to be composed of substructures called systems. It also has been suggested that *structure* be used for the important bare bones of social organization rather than for the actual social relations that take place; thus it could serve in formal analysis as a model or abstraction. Even when this suggestion is enthusiastically adopted, the difference in actual practice is not so very great. If one pictures a descriptive-analytical continuum starting with observed social relations and ending with a formal structural analysis, a piece of professional work falling at any point along the way is likely to be called by some anthropologists a work on any or all of the three topics—"structure," "system," or "organization"—with an occasional "pattern" thrown in.

The relationships of any of the constituent parts of a society or culture to the other parts can be described, just as the dietary pattern of the Siriono was described in terms of their procuring, sharing, cooking, and serving food. When a pattern is analyzed, however, one wants to know how the parts are related, and what happens to the other parts if one is changed in some way. These parts include all elements of the culture, any learned behavior or belief, not only those pertaining to structure. *Function* is the word commonly used for a relationship of interdependence, and the function of any cultural element—social structure, techniques, beliefs, values—may be discerned in the way that it affects other elements and the whole which they make up. Function describes how the society works.

The impressive diversity of the cultural patterns that man has developed to deal with his world has been indicated in the previous section. This section elaborates on variation in social structures and the functions that cultural elements perform.

HOW SOCIETY IS MADE UP

Social structure is the way that individuals in a society are placed and grouped, how they are sorted out. It is composed of statuses and roles, status sectors, social groups, social systems, and the multitude of connections between each of these in a society.

The position of any individual vis-à-vis another person or group is called his status, and since there are many interpersonal and intergroup relationships, each individual occupies a whole host of statuses—rich man, poor man, beggar man, thief, and on through the jingle, being only a minute sample of those available. Even within his family a man may have the several statuses of husband, father, son, brother, son-in-law, each requiring different ways of behaving; within the wider community the possibilities are enormously expanded. The behavior associated with or appropriate to a status is called a role, and each individual, in accordance with his several statuses, has a variety of roles to play. Obviously not all occupants of the same status in a society—father, for example—behave identically; people act their roles with individuality. Nevertheless, within any one culture certain behavior patterns are common to any status.

Relations between people (hence status and role) are characterized by different rights and duties with respect to one another, and by varying degrees of ease or familiarity, power, rank, and prestige. This last characteristic has become, at least popularly, the tail that wags the dog. The easiest way to think of the sum of an individual's multiple statuses—to arrive at *a* status in the society—is to add up the prestige accruing to each. The result is the common expression "high status," or even simply "status." This is merely shorthand for a status with high prestige and leaves important other things about position unsaid.

A status in a society endures as long as it is customarily recognized, while the particular individuals occupying it come and go. Some statuses are ascribed or assigned, such as those determined by sex and age, and birth and inheritance, and others are achieved by the development of particular skills or abilities. For example, any kinship system or military hierarchy is made up of a number of set statuses, such as son, father, cousin, and uncle, or private, sergeant, lieutenant, and general. As they move through their life cycles, individuals are ascribed and so occupy various positions in a kinship system, and in an army different individuals may achieve advancement and so occupy higher ranking positions.

Many aspects of status and role can vary from society to society. Positions conventionally recognized in some cultures include many strange to our own: the *berdache* of some northern Asian and North American Indian tribes, who are men dressed as women, doing women's work, and socially accepted as women; Amazons, crack female troops of the old Dahomean kings; *compadres* in Quintana Roo in Mexico, co-parents with the biological parents, who have strong ties with the biological parents and the child by virtue of both baptismal and pagan rites of godparenthood; the Japanese *baishakunin*, marriage go-betweens for the families involved. The list of culturally defined occupations and relationships can be extended indefinitely.

Even when societies recognize similar statuses, the assigned roles may differ widely. Again the father serves as an example. Malinowski demonstrated that the father in Trobriand Island society was socially defined as the husband of the mother of the child, since these people attributed conception to supernatural rather than natural causes. Properly, one should say that the status of father as we define it did not exist at all, a comparatively rare circumstance in world cultures. But the Trobrianders assigned a role to this "father" like that found in many other societies which, like theirs, were matrilineal. The Trobriand child inherited his name and property from his mother's brother and was also formally instructed by him. The role of the father, in this and other cases, was permissive and affectionate but not responsible.

Other people have even more unique arrangements, but in each case the role of the father as culturally defined fits in with the rest of the social structure. The warrior Nayar castes of Kerala, in southern India, are famous in anthropological literature for the purely biological and legitimizing role of the fathers. As described by Kathleen Gough in a study of matrilineal cultures,[19] Nayar girls before puberty were married by a tali-tying ceremony—in which gold ornaments were tied around their necks—to male representatives of associated lineages. After staying with the brides a few days, these men had no further obligation to them, and they, only slight ritual obligations to the men. The girls, although they remained in their matrilineal households, were then free to take husbands from the associated lineages, who visited them but did not live with them. When a child was born, one of the visiting husbands made a ritual payment to the midwife which legitimized the child. This was the father's only formal social role in regard to the child, although the child owed some respect to both the tali-tier and the midwife-payer. The most obvious contrast with the Nayar "father" is the father in the traditional patrilineal and patriarchal Chinese family. There the father had power, rank, and responsibility which he never lost until death, and even then his prestige survived as he became a revered ancestor.

Other members of the family constellation—sons and mothers-in-law, sisters and brothers—play a range of roles over the globe, from an easy familiarity, through respect and diffidence, to a complete avoidance, so that a Navaho son-in-law, for example, will turn from the path and avert his face to avoid confronting his wife's mother. A large number of cultures have practiced strict mother-in-law avoidance. In a few societies, however—including the Kaingang—a son-in-law might carry familiarity with his mother-in-law to the point of marriage, so that she and her daughter would become co-wives.

Change of status, too, is variously permitted and variously marked from society to society. In some places status is rigidly prescribed; in others there is more mobility. In some places kinship, sex, and advancing years primarily determine status; in others heredity or individual achievement is considered the key to taking on new tasks and prerogatives. Assumption of new positions, however arrived at, may be ceremonially marked. For example, rites of passage—the details of which make up a considerable body of the ethnographical lore—may mark the life crises of birth, marriage, and death, and the important transition from childhood to social adulthood, which is sometimes set at puberty but more often at a culturally selected age. The badges of status such as scarification, circumcision, or other body mutilations may be acquired during these rites, or hairdress or other personal adornment may indicate a new status of marriageability. The variations abound.

Some positions in a society are unique and important (the King) and others are unique and less important (the Keeper of the Royal Umbilical Cord), but most statuses are multiple; that is, numerous people occupy the same position at the same time. They form sectors of society made up of people in the same social category, and whether these people ever come together as a group or not, they may be very important in the work of the society. Sex and age status sectors are the most common examples, since all societies divide their labor by sex and all societies mark stages in the life cycle in some way. Other status sectors cutting across whole communities are class, caste, and slavery, which may be based on a whole range of criteria, including hereditary nobility, wealth, occupation, birth, and captivity. This kind of social stratification, involving subordination of some sectors of the society to others, may be minimal, as among small hunting bands, or extreme, as in some of the great African and European kingdoms. And it may be quite rigid, with marriage permitted only within each sector (endogamy), as in the Hindu caste system, or somewhat less rigid, as in the American class system.

Possible variations in social stratification and mobility are numerous. One of the most unusual arrangements was found among the Natchez Indians of the lower Mississippi. This society was stratified into three classes of nobility—the royal family or Suns, the Nobles, and a lower but still noble class called the Honored People—and the commoners or Stinkards. It was mandatory that marriage of any member of the three upper classes be with a Stinkard, with the children of those unions belonging to the mother's class if she were of the nobility or to the next class below the father's if he were of the nobility. (Some anthropologists have objected that this system could not have prevailed, for the society would eventually have run out of commoners. But others have suggested the supply of Stinkards could have been replenished by the custom prevalent in the area of wholesale adoptions from enemy captives and satellite tribes.)

Social groups, unlike the status sectors of society, are organized aggregations of individuals having face-to-face contact, or of people who are likely to have such contact. Some of these, of course, involve emphasis on similarity of status, as in mothers' clubs, age-graded groups, and warrior societies; but others much more importantly involve complementary rather than similar roles. The family is an important social group and so are its extensions into households or other kindred groups. Clubs and cliques, teams and gangs, small groups brought together to accomplish some particular purpose at work or elsewhere in the community, the community itself, whether it be nomadic band, village, or neighborhood, are all examples of social groups. As diverse as these groups are both within and between societies, they provide the theatre for experience and social action everywhere.

Francis Hsu, an anthropologist who has turned his attention from small local communities to nationalities, has pointed out the relative importance of different social groups in traditional China, Hindu India, and the United States.[20] In China, the family together with its extension into the clan was the dominant group. Here the important relationship was that between father and son, and filial piety, mutual dependence, and continuity of tradition were strong. Hsu describes the Hindu family, on the other hand, as being oriented around the mother-son relationship, and the dominant organizing principle of Hindu society as being hierarchical, as expressed in castes, rather than familial. The American organizing principle he describes as contractual—one of free association—with the club assuming the primacy achieved by the family in China and by caste in India.

People are also bound together by social systems, complex networks of relationships through which individuals are linked with one another, but which never bring them all together as a whole. These systems include kinship ties beyond the local group, such economic activities as marketing or banking, political and governmental interconnections, educational systems, and others which run throughout a society and from society to society. All of the individuals involved in them have certain positions, one linked to another by an activity or interest, but they do not come together as a group and are often even unaware of some other parts of the system. The famous kula ring of the Trobriand Islands serves as an example, partly because of its simplicity and partly because it is less familiar than such systems as, for instance, the complex trading networks of urban Western society. The Trobriand Islanders and neighboring peoples in the South Pacific engaged in a traditional exchange of red shell necklaces moving in one direction through a chain of island communities and white shell bracelets moving in the other. These exchanges were often accompanied by regular trading of goods, but the kula valuables themselves—the necklaces and bracelets—were treasured for their ceremonial and social meaning. Each item had particular mythical and magical associations, its history was known, and all were passed on or received from particular partners. A man might have several kula partners, some to whom he passed the necklaces and from whom he received the bracelets and others with whom the exchange was reversed. Because he met these people with attendant ceremony at frequent intervals and because of their reciprocal obligations, his social relationships with his partners loomed large in his life. Essential as the other links in the kula ring were to the continued working of the system, he never came in contact with those that were outside of his own local group and the groups within which his partners in either direction lived.

In general, status positions are organized into social sectors, groups and systems that crisscross throughout a society and interlink in ways that form the whole social structure. A clearer idea of structure as a whole instead of in fragments may be gained by a glimpse at how two particular societies were made up. The Siriono and the rural Irish serve as examples.

The basic working and social unit of Siriono social structure was the family, composed of a man, his wife (or, more rarely, wives), and their children. They hung their hammocks together in the band's communal hut surrounding the family cooking hearths, planted and tended gardens together, collected food together with or without the man, and in general relied on one another for all the necessities of life. The man was undisputed head of the family, and when there was more than one wife, the first enjoyed privilege and authority. Families related by descent in the female line lived grouped near one another in the band's large hut, cooperated in the various food-getting pursuits and exchanged—reluctantly—the fruits of their labor. The oldest active man in this extended family was usually its leader, but he was not so recognized formally.

Several related extended families lived together in a band, travelling together and only occasionally having any contact with other bands. They occupied the one dwelling, with the chief and his family in the center space. The band generally stayed together during the wet season, but during the dry period families would break away for long hunting and food-foraging trips. There was no specialization of occupation or interest within the band except for that based on sex and age and for the position of chief, which carried with it the obligation to "know more about things and...do them better than anyone else," but not much in the way of prerogatives. Chieftainship passed from father to son if there was one eligible by virtue of his ability. The prestige of any band member depended on performance—mostly in regard to food procurement—and the old people suffered accordingly. Rites of passage were minimal, but parenthood was marked by scarring of the arms.

The Siriono kinship system laced together most of the band because marriage partners were usually selected from within it, and hence everyone was likely to be related to everyone else in some way. The same kinship term was used for many different biological and in-law relationships. Most important from the point of view of behavior patterns, fathers and fathers' brothers, and mothers and mothers' sisters were classed together; children of each of these groups (parallel cousins) were considered as siblings. In contrast, the children of mothers' brothers and fathers' sisters (cross-cousins) were not considered as siblings; indeed, a daughter in the former case and a son in the latter were considered potential mates and called by a term so indicating. There was a free and easy relationship, extending to sexual access, between these potential spouses, and a marked reserve in the relations between siblings and parallel cousins of the opposite sex, who, of course, were not eligible mates.

This is a sketchy description for even a simple social structure, devoid of the details, illustrations, and anecdotes with which ethnographers imbue their descriptions with life. But the description could be even terser: in anthropological shorthand, the bare bones of Siriono social structure consisted of monogamous nuclear and polygynous composite patripotestal families; matrilineal and matrilocal extended families; endogamous bands which were unstratified and occupationally undifferentiated except for sex, age, and patrilineal chieftainships; and a bifurcate-merging kinship system with preferential cross-cousin marriage of the Crow type.

Because most statuses in nonliterate societies are determined by kinship, the anthropological literature is full of special words (such as appear in the previous paragraph) to describe kinship and rules about lineage, inheritance of property, residence, marriage, and other behavior patterns related to kinship. Social anthropologists and sociologists using participant-observer methods have also studied the social structure of various Euro-American communities, and although these kinship systems would seem complex if described technically, it is not necessary to do so, for they are essentially our own.

One of the earliest of these studies was made by Conrad Arensberg and Solon Kimball in the 1930's in rural Ireland. Their interest was in the interaction of custom and social behavior among the small farmers there.[21] They found relationships of the Irish countryman to be dominated by family and community. The nuclear family, living on and deriving its subsistence from its small holding, was the center of organized life. The farmer-father was the head of the family, making the decisions, directing the labor of the other family members, and undertaking the field work and other heavy labor himself along with his grown sons. His wife did the day-to-day house chores, milked and churned, fed the small farm animals, and oversaw the work of her daughters and the smaller boys. Sons and daughters stayed with their parents, dependent on and subordinate to them, until quite late in life. Middle-aged men were often still considered the "boys" of the farm family.

This late social adulthood resulted from a pattern of descent and marriage in which only one son—not the eldest, but a chosen one— inherited the house and farm land and the parents and other children were provided for in large part by a settlement made at the time of the marriage of the heir. This "match" was arranged with an eye not only to the character and reputation of the respective families but also to the "fortune" brought by the bride and, on her family's part, on the worth of the farm into which she would marry. Because marriage meant their abdication and the breaking up of the family, the old couple often delayed match-making. The children, then, waited at home until the fateful decision was made about who got the land, and until the marriage arrangement provided the stake with which they could marry or settle elsewhere.

Power and prestige accompanied age, and even after giving the property to the newly married heir, the old couple, who stayed on in the best room in the house, commanded respect and deference both in the family and in the community.

The sister-brother bond was close, and so was that of their children when their farms were within visiting distance. Consequently, both maternal and paternal cousins to two or three degrees removed developed special relationships. These kindred of the same generation, plus a spouse's own kin, united various of the small farms of the countryside in a pattern of "friendliness." This pattern involved reciprocal lending of labor for special farm tasks, help in giving the family festivals marking the important events in the life cycle, and other kinds of cooperation.

Community extended beyond the cooperation based on kinship ties, often to include those who occupied adjacent townlands. Besides the strong ties of "friends," these communities were organized into sex and age-group cliques, the most important of which was a tightly knit group of old men, family heads, who met informally, but at a set time and place. Old age among the small farmers of recognized ability brought with it respect and influence in the community, and it was during their evening gatherings that decisions and opinions affecting the community crystallized. The only other social stratification resulted from a sprinkling of people following occupations other than farming but living in the small-farm area. Such craftsmen, tinkers, or laborers who depended on the community itself for a poor living were a "cut below" the small-farm class, while those with ties with the urban world—shopkeepers, schoolteachers, priests, big farmers—were a "cut above." The rural community was connected with the larger society through emigrated relatives, the parish and its hierarchy, elected councilmen and the political system, and the system of economic exchange that was centered in the weekly local markets and the larger, ritualized fairs. The Irish small farmer, for all of his provincial way of life, had a position in many more systems linking him with outside community structures than did the isolated Siriono hunter. His society was typical of a peasant society anywhere in that each such society forms part of a social and cultural whole of which an urban component makes up the remainder, and in which the urban part contains the learned or "great" traditions of the civilization represented, as opposed to the popular or "little" tradition of the countryside.

In summary, a society is made up of its own distinctive forms of social differentiation, stratification, and organization. These, along with its other characteristic culture patterns, are the ways that have developed throughout its history to get life's work done.

HOW SOCIETY WORKS

The work of societies is twofold: to meet the physical and psychological needs of individuals and to meet societies' own needs for order and maintenance, which are incurred in the first process. Individual and social needs feed back into each other, with both kinds multiplying. In other words, the communication and cooperation necessary to the satisfaction of such basic needs as sustenance, shelter, sex, or security require social and cultural devices which, in turn, initiate a whole host of other individual needs, now culturally created, and then the additional social and cultural devices necessary to their satisfaction—and so the process continues. Each particular society carries on its culturally patterned activities through its social organization to meet these on-going needs. Anthropologists think that each feature in the whole culture pattern and social structure has some part to play in the process, and this they call its function.

Function, then, is the dynamic aspect of culture pattern and social structure. A function of any customary behavior or belief is how it fulfills individual, social, or cultural requirements, how it affects them. Aside from the basic life-giving functions, effects of custom are sometimes described as psychological and sometimes as social. For examples of the former, it has been suggested about the Siriono that magical hunting techniques functioned in their precarious subsistence economy to relieve hunger anxiety, and that the two-party system in our society functions to drain hostility harmlessly. Some accounts of social function dwell on the effect of a custom on the group as a whole. They describe, for instance, how a particular ritual, such as the Sun Dance, for which bands of Plains Indians came together as a tribe, functioned to promote the solidarity of the group and thus to ensure its continuity. Most anthropologists, however, find it more helpful in understanding the social complexities of particular societies—that is, to see how they work—to think of function in terms of the effect of one custom on other customs.

In this more concrete usage, *function* means the connections between the customs making up a pattern of culture. It refers to how following one custom may support or change the practice of another custom; it refers, that is, to how the parts—customs, traits, institutions—are integrated to form the whole pattern. The concept of function on this level of the interdependence of customs skips, for the time being, the difficult problem of relating an intricate series of only partially understood needs to a wide-ranging diversity of culture traits and social institutions in favor of exploring the many different—indeed, unexpected—links between those traits, institutions, and patterns. Such connections are often apparent to the culture-bearers as well as to the ethnographer looking from the inside, but anthropologists have been particularly interested in more subtle connections. Looking from the outside, they have seen that patterns of behavior relate to other patterns in unintended ways, that changes in one pattern have unlooked-for effects on another pattern. The expressed *purpose* of the behavior may or may not be among its multiple *functions,* depending on whether or not that purpose is actually accomplished; for many anthropologists, because of the joy of discovery, the interesting functions are latent ones—unexpressed and unintended.

One of the best demonstrations of the functional integration of a culture was given, without once using the term, by Lauriston Sharp for the Yir Yoront of Australia in a work in which he traced behavior associated with the stone axe throughout their culture.[22] The Yir Yoront made constant use of short-handled polished stone axes in their daily chores. They used them to chop firewood, to make other tools and weapons, to build their huts and other shelters, and in hunting, fishing, and gathering food. The adult men made all of the axes from materials locally available and from stone heads traded, for spears, from hundreds of miles away. Each man had regular trading partners outside of his own territory, links in an exchange system by which goods moved north and south and in which the stone heads were particularly important. Exchanges usually took place amid much festivity at large ceremonial gatherings during the dry season. The older men also owned the axes, and while they had their exclusive use for certain prestige-connected tasks, for the ordinary jobs everybody used them, particularly women, who were obliged to keep the campfires going day and night. Women and children, when they needed an axe, had to borrow one from husband, father, or older brother; and the etiquette of borrowing included bowing to the owner, thus underscoring his dominant role and the subordinate position of the petitioner, even though the axe was loaned as a matter of course. The stone axe was symbolic of a strong sentiment that ran throughout the Yir Yoront value system, the feeling that males were superior and dominant and that masculine concerns were far more important than female concerns. The axe also symbolized the prestige of age among men.

It may be remembered that the world view of the Yir Yoront saw the present as a mirror of the mythical past, and this too involved the stone axes. Every aspect of life—everything natural, cultural, human—was sacredly associated as a totem with one of the clans into which the Yir Yoront were grouped, so that each clan had hundreds of totems which were believed to be unchanged since the beginning of time. The stone axe was particularly important among the Sunlit Cloud Iguana clan. Only its members might take their names from it or from activities associated with it, and only that clan could represent the stone axe in totemic ritual.

Sharp's analysis of axe-associated behavior reveals the dovetailing of basic Yir Yoront culture patterns. From his data, the functional relationships between Yir Yoront stone axe technology and their social structure can be seen, as well as the interrelations between these and their mythology, and between these and their value system. Each pattern of behavior contributed to and bolstered the others to form an integrated whole.

Functional relationships are inferred from studying patterns of culture at a particular point in time. The crucial test of the analysis, however, is to see what happens to other patterns if one is changed. The nature of the interdependence then becomes explicit. The Yir Yoront case offers just such evidence in what happened when the steel axe was introduced into the culture. This axe or hatchet was among the most eagerly received of the assortment of goods made available to the aborigines by Europeans, and it rapidly replaced its stone counterpart. The changes consequent upon this, among other factors, were far-reaching. These changes were not, however, primarily in the Yir Yoront technology where one might expect to find them—the anthropologist assures us that while the axe enabled the people to carry out their tasks more quickly, the tasks themselves remained much the same—but in other areas of life. Because the new axes were acquired from outside sources by younger males and women alike, the whole structure of interpersonal relations based on age, sex, and kinship altered. No longer the sole owners of axes, no longer the recipients of deferential requests to use them, the older men—the husbands and fathers—found their prestige and authority eroded as their wives and children gained new independence. Since it was no longer necessary to fashion the old axes from the material provided by nature, the self-reliance of the older men diminished, and because a central purpose of the trading system was removed, trading partnerships weakened, exchanges at the great ceremonial occasions dwindled, and these occasions themselves lost much of their former interest. The stone axe was symbolic of the value put on masculine concerns, and as the axe itself faded in importance, so did ideas about masculine dominance.

Because the Yir Yoront believed that anything of the present must reflect the past, they tried to account for the steel axe by discovering it to be among the totems of a clan. While the Sunlit Cloud Iguana clan claimed it as a totem by virtue of their association with the stone axe, unfortunately so did the Corpse clan, which possessed as totems ghosts and all things white, hence white men and by extension things pertaining to white men. The mirroring of the present in their ancestral universe became fuzzy, confusing to read, and because of this and similar problems firm faith in their totemic ideology was replaced by uncertainty. Sharp explained that "The steel axe, shifting hopelessly between one clan and the other, is not only replacing the stone axe physically, but is hacking at the supports of the entire culture system." Observing how the technological change from stone to metal affected the Yir Yoront social structure, their view of the world, and the underlying value system which had held these together as a working whole, the anthropologist predicted the inevitable breakdown of Yir Yoront culture.

In tracing these kinds of interrelationships a great deal must be known about any specific culture. In the first place, not only does a particular culture pattern in any one society have multiple effects— some trivial and some significant, some obvious and some obscure— but ostensibly the same pattern in another culture may have different functions, depending on the unique nature of that culture. Needless to say, many societies use the hatchet without the specific effects noted among the Yir Yoront. On the other hand, the same function can be fulfilled by a variety of institutions within any one society, and the variation becomes vast indeed when several societies are considered. For example, the Natchez class system, the Siriono kinship system, and the Hindu caste system had many different functions. Of particular importance among them was the regulation of marriage. The Natchez had to choose mates from among people occupying a specific class status, the Siriono practiced preferential cross-cousin marriage, and the Hindu married within their caste. No matter how distinctive in form were each of these institutions, they were in one respect functionally similar; that is, they had the like effect of regulating marriage.

Anthropologists attempting to answer the question, "What has what effect?" may soon find themselves engaged in the related problem of "What gives rise to what?" How societies work has much to do with how societies change, and explanations of change are discussed in the next section.

Continuity and Change

Diversity in the ways of man raises the question of why people behave so variously. Patterns of behavior are passed on from generation to generation within a single society, and from society to society within shorter time spans. This transmission of patterns within and between cultures involves both continuity and change; innovation can only take place in the context of given, on-going traditions. While at times these traditions seem to overwhelm the forces for change and at other times to succumb to them, culture-sharing actually always partakes of both processes.

The transmission of patterns also involves feed-back effects between individuals and their culture. That is, culture to a large extent shapes individual behavior, and individuals at the same time change their culture. The problem of how people come to behave so variously, then, can be broken down into two parts; one is how each individual becomes the way he is, and the other is how each culture becomes the way it is. The answer to the first centers on learning, and to the second, on adapting. We are concerned at this point with the diversity of ways in which people "become" and with the culture histories that have resulted in such distinct end products.

BECOMING

Since culture is socially learned and not biologically inherited, one becomes a Siriono, a Tzotzil, a Kota, or a Plainville American, by growing up among the Siriono, the Tzotzil, the Kota, or in Plainville, U.S.A. The process of growing up in a particular culture, of assuming its unique habits of thought and behavior, is called enculturation (or socialization if the focus of interest is society rather than culture). *Becoming a Kwoma, Childhood and Tradition in Two North American Tribes, Coming of Age in Samoa*—these and similar titles of anthropological works indicate that the subject of concern is the processes by which each society educates its youth, shapes them in conformity with its own standards of adulthood. Each individual learns by example, experiment, and instruction. He observes and mimics, acts and reacts, listens and responds. Since he is observing, acting, and listening in a particular cultural context, he has literally no alternative but to "become" a certain kind of cultural being.

From birth a child learns how to respond to the cues of his culture from the people immediately around him—first from his family and then from an expanding circle of older people and peers alike. Approval and disapproval, precept and training gradually mold his behavior according to the design of the culture. Like that design, his learning is not piecemeal but all-of-a-piece, a long, hard job of constantly integrating new revelations with old. The day-to-day learning is continually reinforced by the comfort of conforming, by traditional lore and associated ritual, by the assurance that this is the right and natural way to behave.

Again, diversity characterizes the world picture. Since enculturation patterns are made up of who imparts what, how, and when, and the *what* part of the formula includes the whole culture, the variety of the specific details of becoming is as great as the variety of cultures themselves. Important agents of enculturation—the *who*—may be entirely personal or include the mass media; within the family they may be limited to the parents or include a whole host of succoring and demanding adults, and outside the family they may range from informal and intimate groups of one's peers to rigid sequences of formal schooling controlled by adult strangers. Social controls or sanctions—part of the *how*—may be many different forms of indulgence, affection, and reward, deprivation, threat, and fear, teasing, shaming, and ridicule, or physical punishment. "That *whup* was the main thing to school in them days," recalled a Plainville old-timer about the school of his youth. A reminiscing Cheyenne would have no memories of blows; although his elders expected and received respect from a youth, proper behavior was early instilled by gentle affection—and by leaving bawling babies alone in the brush. Some societies have worked out variously elaborated systems of sanctions, backed by formally structured legal, religious, or social institutions, but all rely primarily on the informal approval and disapproval encountered within small social groups everywhere.

Whatever social controls a society may emphasize in the "becoming" process, both learning and teaching are going on. Margaret Mead has pointed out that the distinction between learning and teaching is important and remarked that the significant difference between the idea of education held by South Pacific peoples she has worked among and that held in our own society is ". . .the shift from the need for an individual to *learn* something which everyone agrees he would wish to know, to the will of some individual to *teach* something which it is not agreed that anyone has any desire to know."[23]

Traditional ways, learned during childhood, are emotionally powerful and, in their effect on the individual, go beyond shaping behavior and belief to develop distinctive personality characteristics. Becoming is not simply a matter of accruing custom like layers of paint; it involves the formation of deep-seated traits. Personality results from the interplay of the individual and his culture in two overlapping ways. One is through the admiration and emulation of certain personality types or attributes. The Cheyenne youth, for example, consistently heard courage extolled and always had models of bravery before him. The other way is through a whole complex of situational, cultural, and psychological circumstances. The Siriono seem to have developed an aggressive yet apathetic, individualistic, and uncooperative personality, not because such behavior was particularly admired, but in response to their precarious subsistence, particularly their continuously frustrated hunger drive. The structuring of personality in this way is not simply a matter of conscious and unconscious imitation and learning; it involves other psychological responses to the surrounding world. Paramount in this world are culturally determined modes of child care. Anthropologists in general have collected a great deal of material on child-rearing methods in many different cultures, and some anthropologists especially inter-

ested in the relationship between culture and personality development have tried to relate these methods to personality types in
particular societies. Observation of nursing and weaning practices,
the presence or absence of warm bodily contact, the ways in which
children are fed, played with, taught—of the ways in which they are
treated in general—has been supplemented by the collection of life
histories and the results of a whole battery of projective tests ob-
tained in close collaboration with interested psychologists.

Summaries of two versions of becoming can illustrate variation
both in anthropological approach and in cultural experience. One
is of growing up in Atimelang, a village on the island of Alor in the
East Indies, and the other is of growing up in Peyrane, a village in
the Vaucluse, a department of France.

Cora Du Bois went to Atimelang specifically to describe any personality characteristics common to the villagers and to analyze the
relationship of such characteristics to the culture.[24] She wanted to
discover how cultural pressures operated during the life cycle to produce the basic personality type and how this personality in turn affected Alorese institutions. An interesting aspect of the study was
that her own analysis of the Atimelangers, made within a psycho-
analytic framework, was checked by psychological tests given by her
but interpreted independently. The people Du Bois settled among
lived off the produce of their fields and gardens, supplemented by
meat—mostly pig or rat. Women were charged with the cultivation
and collection of plant foods, and men with carrying on an extremely
complex financial system. This system involved the exchange of pigs,
gongs, and kettledrums primarily in connection with marriage arrangements, burial feasts, and housebuilding, transactions that included elaborate negotiations and were of many years' duration. It
was through skill in these financial dealings that the Atimelang man
acquired not only credit but also prestige.

Child care in Atimelang was casual, training almost nonexistent,
and discipline inconsistent. Babies were generally fondled and made
over by everybody, but soon after birth the mother returned to her
work in the fields leaving the baby with whatever other family members were around—older siblings, perhaps, or the father if he were
not off dunning a debtor or otherwise conducting his financial affairs. Although the mother-substitutes were more or less accepting
of the baby's care, feeding him gruel when he cried with hunger,
from the time his mother returned to her work there was no one consistently available to him as a nurturing figure. Nor did anyone take
on the particular task, as he grew, of shaping his behavior to an ap-

proved pattern. He was not helped to walk or talk, but neither was he pressured into learning other skills and controls; his toilet training was not a matter of great concern, his mishaps in this realm usually being tolerated, and he slept when and where it suited. He learned, as the anthropologist put it, by "absorption"—by absorption and by the inconsistent but restrictive discipline that soon became his lot.

After the child learned to walk, his care became even more off-hand. No longer carried about, he lost, except when sleeping with others, the bodily contact he was used to, including the sexual fondling with which he had been placated as an infant. For the part of the day that his mother worked in the gardens his feeding was erratic and to a large extent consisted of what he could beg from others. Also, the warm-water baths of his infancy were exchanged for cold-water dousings and scrubbings painful to his multiple scratches and lesions from yaws. The small child, helpless in the face of neglect and these discomforts, cried and had temper tantrums. These and other offenses that might bother adults were dealt with inconsistently. Du Bois told of one two-year-old boy who flew into a violent rage every morning that his mother left him for the fields, running after her, then rolling around and beating his head on the ground. His mother sometimes ignored him completely, continuing on her way. Or sometimes she returned to comfort him, or to slap him, or to stay with him until she could slip away later. Mostly, however, children were disciplined by blows, by frightening them with bogeymen, and by teasing and shaming. Rarely were rewards promised for good behavior and—the anthropologist pointed out—even more rarely were such promises kept.

As the children grew older they gave up their tantrums for other ways of dealing with their world. Girls were trained in the food production sphere of their mothers—incidentally getting to eat better and oftener than before. The boys were left to fend for themselves, and did so by foraging food from the gardens and fields, hunting rats, exchanging favors for food, and stealing. Boys and girls alike played much of the time, imitating the pursuits of their elders. Childish aggression was channeled into verbal rather than physical expression. Discipline became harsher, with blows meted out by almost any irritated adult; parents thought nothing of confiscating their children's property; and ridicule and deception were used not only to control the children but also for the amusement it might give the perpetrator. So ingrained were teasing and deceiving that lying was completely accepted—Du Bois comments that the remark, "You lie," was considered to be simply a statement of fact, not an insult or a reproach. Sexual activity among the children and adolescents was not encouraged, but neither was it harshly treated. The passage to adulthood was as casual as was their whole childhood. When and if they felt like it the girls got tatooed, the boys let their hair grow, and both groups filed and blackened their teeth. They did these things not for reasons of ritual but for beauty's sake.

Du Bois and the psychologists collaborating with her describe the basic personality of the people of Atimelang as being characterized by a sense of confusion and futility because of the inconsistency of their treatment; by resentment, anxiety, and suspiciousness because of the way they were frustrated and deceived; and by lack of self-confidence and self-esteem because they were not trained with praise, encouragement, and reward. Atimelangers did not trust others and seemed unable to form warm and stable interpersonal relationships, remaining self-contained, internally isolated. Neither did they trust themselves; self-assurance or positive and responsible attitudes were not developed. Shaming and teasing left them feeling hostile and aggressive, but without the resources to organize these feelings into self-reliant action. Ambivalence toward the mother, who both gratified and frustrated their hunger and sexual tensions, carried over into marriage relations, which were precarious. Desertion, infidelity, and divorce were commonplace.

This basic personality not only resulted from cultural patterns of child care, but also contributed in turn to the perpetuation of those patterns and, indeed, fit in with much of the rest of Atimelang social life. Men had to enter the financial system in order to get the worldly goods necessary for both marriage and the proper propitiation of their dead kin, who would otherwise be dangerous to them. Within the financial system, in the competition for wealth and prestige, they found a culturally approved channel for their diffuse aggressive feelings as well as a field for the tactics of trickery and deception with which they had been familiar since infancy. Other culturally sanctioned outlets for hostility were internal quarrels and external wars, but, as in child rearing, verbal onslaughts were much preferred and physical attacks, which in the past had led to protracted headhunting feuds, were restrained. Handicrafts were done carelessly on the whole, perhaps because rewards for success had been scant throughout their lives. Religious ceremony consisted mostly of placating supernatural beings with sacrifices of food, made reluctantly, only in response to social pressure—much, the anthropologist thought, as the child conformed, unwillingly, in the face of superior force.

With a purpose more general than the one Du Bois set herself, Laurence Wylie went to the Vaucluse because he wanted to give "a reasonably accurate idea" of life in a French village. The concepts and methods that he used in his field work and analysis were not explicitly psychological although some of his speculations about personality development were. His study includes a vivid account of how the children of Peyrane became the adults of Peyrane.[25] Liberally larded with anecdotes about personalities, his description of the culture is organized around the life cycle. Peyrane was a community of small farmers and villagers in southern France. Its people were well aware of their many ties to and dependency on the outside world, but they thought of them as seldom as possible, focussing the great burden of their interest and energies inward on their own families.

The care and training of children in Peyrane was directed toward a steady development of self-control and a stoical acceptance of life's hardships, both at considerable expense to self-expression. Babies were affectionately and indulgently treated, swaddled for one or a few months after birth, fed when hungry, cleaned when dirty, comforted when crying, and proudly displayed for public admiration. If the mother had to work away from her child, willing relatives or neighbors took over his care for that time. Weaning, walking, toilet training, and correct behavior were all accomplished gradually with the patient help of elders. Formal polite behavior toward adults was insisted upon, and this insistence was reinforced daily with rewards of candy and cookies. Insults and verbal abuse were permitted among children—sometimes spilling over, at a safe distance, to adults—but fighting was not. Even very young children were expected to help out with chores and, when playing, to be careful of themselves and their toys, and to remain clean. Conformance was achieved mostly through encouragement and explanation, but when these failed, culprits were shamed, ridiculed, threatened, and, more rarely, punished with blows.

At school, entered at age four, the home training was continued, with greater demands, more rigid treatment, and harsher discipline. The people of Peyrane considered schooling a very necessary and serious affair, and they expected their children to measure up to school responsibilities. Parents and teachers cooperated throughout the school years, forcing the children to conform in their personal conduct ("One does what is expected! That's the way it is!") and to meet scholastic expectations—expectations which, however, were adjusted to openly assessed individual capabilities ("There's an intelligent little one. . . . .It's a pleasure to teach a child like that." "There's Renée. Not stupid, but lazy." "Poor Marie. She tries, but. . . .").

For the first one or two years of school the children learned submission to the formal school situation and classroom decorum. Then they were engaged in reading, writing, and arithmetic, later supplemented by history and geography and a smattering of practical science. The curriculum also included the daily learning of some moral precept, illustrated by a story. Throughout, great stress was put on politeness, neatness, and not endangering life or limb. Importantly, a whole way of thinking, an approach to life, was inculcated by the teaching method that was used consistently. This method was the memorization of a rule or principle, its illustration by concrete facts, and practice in its use to solve set problems. The student's own curiosity and sense of discovery were not encouraged. The teaching also stressed, implicitly if not explicitly, that all facts fit into a larger framework and that the important facts were those practically relevant to daily experience.

As the parents at home used both rewards and punishment in pressuring the children to conform, so did the teachers at school. For example, there was a prize-awarding ceremony to close the school year, at which every child won some kind of prize, and throughout the year colored prints, candy, and other favors were given for merit. Punishment, in general, was made to fit the offense, such as having to sit still for restlessness, redoing homework for mistakes or sloppiness, and so on. Shaming, however, was the standard punishment for all kinds of infractions, the teacher's sharply critical tongue and the derision of onlookers combining to isolate the wrongdoer in his misery. Wylie recounts how a boy who turned in sloppy school work had it pinned to his back for all to mock him as he walked through the village from school to church, for his catechism class; and how a little girl who stole money for gum from her father, besides the punishment assured her at home, was made to walk in a circle during recess, with her hands on her head and a sign proclaiming her a thief pinned to her back, as the other children taunted her.

At fourteen, the children left school molded to accept docilely and passively the social code and way of life in Peyrane. For a few years they were relatively free, usually supporting themselves, and expected to have a good time—the boys, to sow a few wild oats—before settling down to raise their own families.

Family life was the center of existence, and individuals took some initiative in acting constructively for the family's welfare. Not so in other spheres. Wylie speculates that the relationship of the people with their government paralleled their school experience: trained in school to repress spontaneity and initiative, they did not try to work for the welfare of the community by cooperative or constructive political action; having been acted upon in school, they felt that they were manipulated by the government rather than participants in it; resigned to the rigidity of school life, they remained resigned to their powerlessness in later life; scorned and shamed when their behavior deviated from the acceptable, they outwardly conformed and inwardly became convinced that organized human power was malevolent and society hostile. In their political behavior, the basically conservative people of Peyrane tended to figuratively thumb their noses at power—the government—many of them by not voting at all or by voting extremist anti-government tickets.

In discussing enculturation and personality formation, the words *shape* and *mold* have been used loosely to describe a cultural effect, not to deny individual variability due to inherited temperament or ability and personal experience. The power of tradition is enfolding, but it is not a straitjacket. Alternative ways of behaving exist within any culture, and where there is culture contact, there is still wider scope for selection of behavior. Again, when new situations occur, there are even more options. Even as the child is being enculturated, as tradition is perpetuated, individual choices and other patterns transmitted from outside the culture may transform it.

Diffusion of patterns from one culture to another in situations of prolonged close contact is called acculturation. Acculturation, like enculturation, refers to the taking-on by individuals of distinctive ways of behaving, but in this case the transfer is cross-cultural instead of cross-generational and new ways are introduced instead of old ways perpetuated.

Although anthropologists have become increasingly interested in the hows and whys of social and cultural change, one of their most important contributions to understanding other people has been to look past surface acculturation to the persistence of traditional values and ways of thinking learned in childhood. People may change their mode of dress, shelter, technology, and even language relatively easily, while other characteristics are more resistant to modification. For example, the sociologist Herbert Gans, who studied an Italian community of "urban villagers" in the West End of Boston, discovered that the second generation had little or no interest in the old country and that, except for food habits and to some extent language, there seemed to be little carry-over of Italian culture patterns.[26] Fuller investigation, however, revealed that there was an outstanding exception to the apparent lack of persistence of tradition, and this was their social structure. The second generation was organized along the same lines as the first: the family circle was important, friendships made during childhood were lasting, there was segregation by sex

and age, and peer-group associations were paramount—so much so
that Gans epitomized the West Enders as "peer group society." The
traditional social structure had survived the loss of other culture patterns.

There is interesting evidence that some groups have retained their
basic personality structure in spite of acculturation on other levels.
Gans was interested in social structure and so explained West End
phenomena in those terms, but the structure he described must inevitably have been part of cultural sets deeply rooted in West End
personality patterns. Anthropologists working with American Indians of varying degrees of acculturation have repeatedly attested to
their fundamental "Indian-ness," much of which they describe as
consisting of strong inner control of aggression and emotional re-
straint in general. The anthropologist A. Irving Hallowell, working
among acculturated Ojibwa Indians, discovered that they were "still
Ojibwa in a psychological sense whatever their clothes, their houses,
or their occupations, whether they speak English or not, and regardless of race mixture."[27] The typical Ojibwa personality was intro-
verted, restrained, and on the surface amiable while inwardly anx-
ious and suspicious. This structure, Hallowell points out, was suited
to the aboriginal culture, which held that the good in life depended
on supernatural help, achieved by fasting and dreams, and that harm
came from sorcery practiced by one's fellow man. The Ojibwa personality derived security from Ojibwa religious beliefs and functioned to avoid provoking other men to retaliatory anger.

Among one highly acculturated group of Ojibwa, Hallowell found
the basic personality structure still evident but no longer appropriate to its cultural context. The supporting religious beliefs were gone
and no other meaningful values or goals had been substituted. Internal control of aggression in interpersonal relations was still present,
but it increasingly broke down and inner confusion led to apathetic
behavior. In this case, in Hallowell's words, "a high level of acculturation conceal[ed] a psychological skeleton." Louise and George
Spindler, studying the Menominee Indians, made much the same
finding of persistence of the basic personality structure, but among
the Menominee the most acculturated Indians had also made the
psychological change, incorporating a personality structure compatible with the new culture.[28]

Becoming to a large extent reflects the impact of a culture on an individual. When the process of change is examined, emphasis shifts
to the impact of the individual on his culture.

CHANGING

In 1961 the supervision of the affairs of the Menominee Indians was removed from the Bureau of Indian Affairs, and their reservation was made into a county of the state of Wisconsin. The "vanishing Indian" had not vanished, but he most certainly had changed, and Congress, in terminating the special Federal status of the Menominee, was setting in motion even further changes. The termination decision was unpopular among the Menominee because it added many direct hardships to an already far from easy existence, and it prompted them to express a wide range of concerns about the future. Their concerns and opinions related to their economy, their particular way of life, and their relations with the non-Menominee world. Among these expressions, publicized in a television documentary, was that of an adult Menominee who, although he had no panacea for his tribe's problems, did have a framework within which to consider them. "When it comes to social and economic advantage," he stated bluntly and earnestly, "I say, dump the culture!"

This colloquial expression of opinion is a capsule illustration of why cultures change. People try to deal more satisfactorily with existing conditions, and they make adjustments to changing conditions. Through their culture, people adapt to their natural, social, and—most important—their cultural environment. This by no means implies that all adaptations are for the best, as we would view the best, but only that they have sufficient success under specific conditions for currency. Nor are culture patterns so easily abandoned as the Menominee quoted would have it, as has already been indicated. Culture change is initiated in social action. It starts out with people opting for certain behavior, and if that behavior is comparatively satisfying, it will be adopted by still others. It has been usual to speak of such shared behavior as part of culture only when it has persisted from generation to generation, when it has become part of the body of tradition or design for living of a people. But culture has always been transmitted horizontally, too—that is, borrowed from other cultures. The rapid technological and social transformations of today have increased that dimension of culture change.

Culture patterns and social structures are frequently described as if caught at a particular point of time, as if all their parts were in balance. This, however, is only a convenient fiction. The investigator knows that culture is not static, but dynamic; he knows that within the given patterns and structures people are choosing ways of acting, and that these choices change, whether gradually or swiftly, the total pattern of the culture.

People make choices in particular surroundings and in particular circumstances. The surroundings include man's self-created environment—his society and his culture—as well as the natural environment—topography, climate, and the plant and animal world; and the circumstances include historical ones as well as the immediate situation. In other words, the innovation and acceptance of new culture traits, the elimination of old, and the mutual adjustment or modification of the old and the new, take place in specific ecological, historical, functional, and situational contexts. Anthropologists studying culture change have found it advantageous to take into account all of these overlapping contexts, whether their main interest has been in the history or in the functioning of a particular culture. There are many diverse cultures in the world because every culture is the product of a unique series of events taking place in unique surroundings. To understand how any one of these cultures came to have its particular form one needs to know its total ecology at various points in time—to know, that is, the relationship between the environment and the cultural adaptations to it. Adaptation to the environment must be a continuous process because the environment itself changes. Gradual or cataclysmic changes in nature, population variations or movements, and above all, culture change itself cause more culture change, as each adaptation in turn becomes part of the whole environment. Included in what one needs to know to understand how any culture became crystallized, then, is its culture history (the sequence of ideas and institutions developed within the culture or borrowed from other cultures) and its functional integration (how in this sequence culture elements were interrelated, how each affected the others).

A culture history study describes the materials used in culture building, the innovations made and accepted by the group. Any innovation in thinking or behaving is a new synthesis of elements already present in the culture or in cultures with which there is contact. Therefore, both the stock of accumulated knowledge and relationships with other cultures help explain change in any particular culture. Innovations are more often borrowed than independently made, success in one culture being a prime incentive to the people of another culture. This is evident throughout world culture history, at least since prehistoric men began to match their stone tools and weapons against their neighbor's metal ones, until the world-wide demand today for the devices and products of Western technology. Even when an idea is not borrowed directly, it may be stimulated by like ideas in other cultures, as was the case when writing, but not a particular alphabet, spread from Mesopotamia to Egypt, or as may have been the case when the Iroquois confederacy offered an example for political organization to the rebellious American colonies. Because of the surpassing importance of borrowing in culture building, slowness of change and degree of isolation go hand in hand.

Culture change is cumulative in the sense that knowledge depends on prior knowledge; certain innovations cannot be made if others have not been made before them. Technological change is the most obvious example of this. The present fantastic array of computers, power tools, other industrial gadgetry, and weaponry have developed on the basis of earlier inventions or borrowings of techniques and materials, and these on still earlier ones—to greatly oversimplify, the wheel and the combustion engine had to come before the car. Culture is cumulative in other realms of life, too, however. Forms of ritual and political organization, styles of literature, scientific methods, and philosophical theorizing have all built on innovative thinking of the past. Because new ideas and ways of behaving are combinations or recombinations of elements already present in the culture, or in cultures with which there is contact, the cultural inventory— that is, the cultural baggage carried by any group of people—both provides the basis for change and limits that change. Some kinds of change are not cumulative, however, but limited by constricted sets of possibilities. There are only so many ways to classify kin, for example, only so many criteria to use in establishing residence, or only so many ways to reckon descent.

The cultural inventory may be inhibiting to change in yet another way; values or world views may be directly antithetical to change. Again the Yir Yoront are a useful illustration. At the time of the anthropologist's stay with them, in their frequent traffic on the local waterways they used only a light log to which they clung while swimming. This exposed them to pain, even mortal danger, from the many menacing inhabitants of those waters and precluded the possibility of deep-water fishing. Yet not far away were other tribes successfully making and using bark canoes, and the materials for making them were also available to the Yir Yoront. Sharp explains that while the technological change would have been an easy one to achieve, the world view of the Yir Yoront was an obstacle. The bark canoe, they assumed, was part of the mythical past of their neighbors, but it was not part of their own ancestral universe. No bark canoe in their totemic ideology, no bark canoe for them—not, anyway, until someone invented and others accepted a myth to account for bark canoes, which was a far more difficult undertaking than the mere fashioning of a canoe. Even though the steel axe had its stone predecessor and its association with white men-ghosts to ease its way, it, too, was not clearly accounted for mythically; and therefore its adoption weakened the ideological system.

This kind of thinking in a people's cultural repertory is not the same thing as reluctance to change, which may occur even in societies with a strong commitment to change, where the idea of progress and the perfectibility of man and his works is part of the value system. The "isolated" and "backward" Plainville of James West's study loudly and proudly resisted government-sponsored reform of local farming practices even while scientific farming gradually became accepted. Fifteen years later another investigator found Plainville so dependent on urban ways of life that change was no longer resisted but anticipated.[29]

The cultural inventory includes, then, not only knowledge and skills but values and ideas, and it provides the context within which individuals vary in the choices they make. Even the most tradition-bound culture offers alternative ways of behaving. Not all Cheyenne youths felt the role of the archetypal brave warrior to be congenial; some chose other models. Not all—or even most—of the sons of the Plainville farmer settled down to become home folk; many migrated to town or city. The frequency of certain choices made from the various ones available may shift the real culture ("the work made") further and further from the culture norms ("the design"), until the design itself changes. West wrote that cooperative help among closely related families in Plainville was voiced as an ideal, although in fact it was considerably eroded in both practice and thought. Gallaher, the anthropologist who followed West to the community, found that by then independence from kin and neighbors was considered a positive virtue; it was thought best not to depend on others for help—and best not to have to help them. Even close relatives living near one another might duplicate expensive farm machinery, more for prestige than for practical reasons. When innovations, cultural alternatives, and individual variability are considered, one can see why the idea of culture as a mold, while useful as a general concept, should not be taken as literal in detail.

Pattern and function help explain both the selection of new ways and the further modifications of the culture when such ways are adopted. Looking from the inside, an innovation is accepted if it appears rewarding in some way, either because of the usefulness of the innovation itself or because of the prestige awarded the innovators and their imitators. It is more likely to be accepted if it is compatible with existing patterns of behavior—it is usually easier for a culture to borrow from a similar culture. But if the rewards are high enough or the penalties for not accepting uncomfortable enough, new ideas are adopted that are not consistent, or even conflict, with the old. The new way may be altered to fit better with other patterns, and in turn is likely to cause changes in them, just as the steel axe led to changes in Yir Yoront social organization and ideology.

Since innovations, trivial or basic, are constantly occurring in any society, cultures are never perfectly integrated or consistent. Conflict exists and modifications are made that lead to further modifications, not in an orderly chain of development but in a spiraling meshwork of unexpected developments. To say that people modify their culture in this way is the same thing as to say that culture patterns are interdependent and helps explain how a culture adapts to its whole environment—or, as happens when the strains become too severe, suffers disintegration.

Understanding how cultures change and how cultures function are closely related endeavors. Subsistence patterns, social structure, and value systems interrelate and change one another. The advent of the horse on the Plains and the car in Plainville may serve as starting points for specific examples. The eagle-feathered, horse-riding warrior and buffalo hunter of the Great Plains typifies, for most people, the American Indian. Yet the horse was introduced to Indian culture via the Spanish explorers of the Southwest and was not fully integrated into Cheyenne life, for example, until the last half of the eighteenth century. The particular history of the Cheyenne differs in detail from that of other Plains tribes, but their story nevertheless illuminates the more general one of groups formerly marginal to the Plains acquiring the horse, moving out onto the Plains, and adapting their whole style of life to conditions there.

According to archaeological and historical evidence, the Cheyenne once lived in earth lodge villages along tributaries of the Missouri River, in a grassy plains region also occupied by other sedentary village tribes. Here the women tended gardens, growing corn, beans, and squash, and the men hunted and defended the group from enemies. The diffusion of patterns of culture related to the horse—their use in hunting and in war, how they were stolen or traded and cared for, the gear used in riding and in transporting belongings—has been told in many studies of Plains culture. Suffice it to say that the Cheyenne, through contact with other Indian cultures, also acquired horses. Drawn by the advantages to buffalo hunting accruing from this new mobility, and perhaps pushed westward by enemies to the east, the tribe gave up its settled, farming existence for the nomadic, hunting life of the Plains.

Combining the historical and functional approaches, the social anthropologist Fred Eggan has demonstrated how Cheyenne society adapted to Great Plains ecology by comparing their life there with their earlier life in the villages, using as a general model for the latter the subsistence patterns and social structure of the tribes that remained in the earth lodge villages along the Missouri.[30] The Cheyenne adapted swiftly to a life of almost total dependence—for food, clothes, and shelter—on the buffalo of the Plains. The new subsistence conditions to which they had to adjust were the habits of the migratory buffalo, which scattered during the part of the year when provender was hard to come by, and gathered during the summer mating season, when grass became lush enough to support the united herd. Correspondingly, during most of the year the Cheyenne were organized in a number of scattered camping and hunting bands, which then joined together in the summer for tribal ceremonies and the communal hunt.

Buffalo hunting and constant warfare, with tribes competing for hunting regions and raiding each other for horses, made flexibility of organization imperative for success. The necessary flexibility was partly achieved by giving up the lineage system of organization practiced in the villages, whereby descent was reckoned through the mother and the operating extended family unit cut through the generations, and by adopting a grouping based on belonging to the same generation and the cooperation of "brothers," with both sides of the family equally recognized. The bands so formed were usually made up of the families of siblings, close relatives, and friends, who followed a leader who, far from inheriting his status as the village chiefs usually did, had continually to prove himself in war and the hunt. Courage in war was glorified, and horse-raiding brought prestige as well as the more tangible reward. The criteria for leadership, however, included proof as well as promise of success in the band's competitive forays. Anyone was free to join a band or to drop out of it, so the size of a band as well as its leadership depended on success in raiding and hunting.

The flexibility of the bands, which gave them the ability to take action quickly, was contained and ordered within the tribal organization. When the tribe came together during the summer, the bands camped in specific places in a great circle, with a lodge for a council of selected chiefs placed in the center. Tribal organization included, besides this council, a group selected from among the numerous warrior societies to organize and police the communal hunt. During the summer encampment, certain objects sacred to the whole tribe were present and group ceremonies to ensure tribal well-being were held. These symbols and rituals served to unify the tribe spiritually.

Significantly, as Eggan points out, other tribes marginal to the Great Plains, whose backgrounds and social systems were different from those of the earth lodge villages, once they were on the Plains also developed the kind of flexible band organization that the Cheyenne did. He explains that "social structures have jobs to do," and that when the task changes, the structure must adapt to the changed situation if the society is to persist.

As the use of horses modified subsistence, social, and value patterns on the Plains, so did the use of cars contribute to a spiral of change in Plainville. The first cars in Plainville appeared in 1912, and although regarded with suspicion or considered "just a passing fad," they were in wide use by 1920, partly because the market for farm produce was good at the time and money was available. In the following decades, highways were built to accommodate the cars, and more cars were bought to fill the highways: Plainville's isolation was ended. The car was used for marketing produce, and new car-connected jobs opened up—servicing, repairing, trucking, and even factory work. At the same time, the old crafts and skills disappeared; even the blacksmith spent most of his time on car and tractor repairs.

Plainville people thought of the car mostly, however, as a social convenience, as they thought of the telephone that preceded and the radio that succeeded it. Patterns of visiting, courting, entertainment, and mutual help were all affected as, able to go further faster and oftener, Plainvillers no longer had to confine exchanges of gossip, meals, work, and other favors to within their neighborhoods. Increased mobility was widely blamed for a decline in neighborliness—it was said that people didn't "visit" or "help" or "borry" or "loan" as they once had. Indeed family bonds and community solidarity weakened as cars allowed people to reach beyond their neighborhoods. For a while, at least, class distinctions were accentuated by the more and better cars of the prairie farmers and the "jalopies" of the hill folk.

The car and the radio too, exposed Plainville people to the goods available and the salesmanship marketing them in the outside world, an exposure already initiated by the mail-order catalog. They needed more money not only to pay the considerable expenses involved in car ownership but also to satisfy the new desires that this increased exposure instilled in them. They became discontented with the traditional values and resources of their own community and accepted more and more the values of the mass urban culture. From the beginning of the century when "no neighbor ever charged anything" in the subsistence economy of the period to the time of West's visit, there was a weakening of cooperative work exchange and purely subsistence farming and an acceptance of the idea of money and a money economy, greatly reinforced by the innovation of car use. By the time of Gallaher's visit, farming was considered not so much a way of life as a business for profit, a means of obtaining money to buy the goods and services the people had learned to require.

In conclusion, in so far as peoples have had distinct ecologies and distinct historical contacts, they have developed distinct cultures through the innovation, selection, and modification of culture traits and patterns.

3

The Universally Human

Mana, tapu, totem, brideprice, couvade, and potlatch were offered as random witnesses to cultural diversity, but these words also testify to the common humanity underlying that diversity. Anthropologists argue about the validity of extending the meaning of terms first used to describe customs in particular cultures to cover similar habits of thought in other cultures, but the argument arises only because the similarities do seem obvious. Mana is a Polynesian concept, but the idea of impersonal power attached to certain objects is found in cultures all over the world. Ritual avoidances called *tapu,* a Polynesian word, are so similar to other worldwide practices that the word *taboo* long ago gained currency—and has been satirically extended. Social anthropologists no longer think of totemism so much as a distinct institution but as a commonplace way of thinking about natural phenomena in terms of human social relationships. The so-called brideprice is one form of the exchange to cement relations between the families of marriage partners that occurs widely, in both technologically simple and technologically complex societies. Elements of the custom called couvade have global distribution, and a psychological couvade—a sharing of the mother's experience—is memorialized in the comic scene in our culture of the fainting father. The potlatch is unique in its details, but it has been seen as a manifestation of conspicuous giving for the sake of prestige, a not-so-rare mode of behavior.

In brief, there are many similarities from culture to culture. Furthermore, beneath even the most diverse behavior certain common sentiments and modes of thought can be discerned. Our interest now turns from exploring the wide range of cultural diversity displayed by mankind to focus on the limits to that diversity, set in part by a universal human nature, and on cultural uniformities or—more likely—similarities. "The mores can make anything right," wrote William Graham Sumner in his famous *Folkways*, referring to morally-binding custom. "But they have a harder time making some things right than others," the sociologist Robert Park used to tell his students. Robert Redfield, in his essay which reports this sequence of remarks, mentions child sacrifice and suttee—the immolation of the widow—as two customs which could not have been easily borne.[1] It is relevant to remember Cora Du Bois' thought that one of the reasons that the Atimelang villagers repressed physical violence in their children and tried as adults to circumvent it was that, in their culture, such conflict could lead to a bloody chain of headhunting episodes. Further, when the government prohibited headhunting, the people complied with noticeable willingness.

Although anthropologists have traditionally been immersed in and intrigued by man's strange customs, and dedicated to understanding them in their cultural context, they have never lost their original vision of anthropology as a comparative study of man. The very discussion of differences assumes a common basis for such differences, and most workers are able to combine their great interest in the unique with concern for questions of similarity and universality. They embark on what one of them has called "the quest for universals." A few still explore the validity of assumptions that man everywhere is basically the same biological creature. By far the most of those engaged in pan-human, cross-cultural research, however, are looking for what man has developed culturally in common, and why.

The Quest for Universals

The quest for universals increasingly motivates cross-cultural research, but its roots are deep in the comparatively brief history of the study of man as a discipline. Early scholars spoke of "the psychic unity of man" or observed that "an obscure psychology underlies social reality." Mysterious "elementary ideas" were thought to be common to mankind, and hence the source of certain culture traits found again and again throughout the world. Furthermore, it was assumed that these traits evolved in a fixed order, and this led to a scheme of stages of cultural development through which groups everywhere were supposed to progress—or stagnate along the way. Lack of reliable data from the field and lack of awareness of the transforming impact of culture contact and the world-spanning effect of diffusion, however, crippled those early efforts to assess the universal nature of man.

Current anthropologists concerned with this question are correcting earlier deficiencies in both gathering data and building theory. They are using many techniques of collecting and storing field data that insure objectivity, critically examining their methodology, and questioning their theoretical assumptions. Participant observation still provides the basic data of anthropology, but increasingly anthropologists are recognizing a need to use counts and statistical analysis to reflect the magnitude of cultural alternatives and deviations from accepted patterns, in order to better understand cultural dynamics. Anthropological method is still primarily that of natural history—field observation, classification, and comparison—but some anthropologists also try to use formal models in the analysis of their data; they experiment with bare-bones models of cultures, deducing what would happen to one part if another part were changed. These new experiments in techniques of analysis do not, however, diminish the search for humanistic insight into the universally human.

From the scientific point of view, the quest is for generalizations about human behavior and the principles governing it. The search can be initiated in two complementary and overlapping ways. One way focusses on cultures, caught at particular points in time and space, as particular cultural solutions to problems posed by life. It deals with *what* man faces. This frame of reference is a counterpoint to the earlier discussion of culture pattern, social structure, and function. The other way adds the dimension of passing time—it focusses on the processes involved in the development of particular cultures. It deals with *how* man faces his problems, and is a counterpoint to the earlier discussion of continuity and change. Both of these approaches to the quest for universals—the one couched in terms of problems and solutions and the other in terms of process and substance—lean heavily on what has been learned of diversity.

PROBLEMS AND SOLUTIONS

The anthropologist away from the field, at work at his desk is faced with making decisions about how to use his material, in conjunction with other data collected by his colleagues, in order to make general propositions about culture. Ironically, since the comparative method is fundamental to the discipline, anthropologists have considerable difficulty in deciding just what to compare. Also, there is a choice to be made as to which of several methods of comparison might be the most fruitful. The decisions are, of course, interconnected.

The anthropologists who were first interested in the quest for universals pointed out that there seemed to be broad areas of life that were comparable from culture to culture. Everywhere people have a language, a way of making a living, a way of organizing to get things done, ideas about the unknown, and so on, all of which can be described under certain headings. A complete list of the headings would include all facets of any culture. This idea of an encompassing, universal pattern stresses similarities in the classification of culture content as opposed to the specific details of each culture—that is, the differentiated content itself. It was soon discovered that although this scheme is effective as a framework for descriptions of cultures, it is not adequate for cross-cultural comparisons except of the most general kind.

Traditionally, anthropologists have compared cultures to determine similarities of social institutions or culture patterns. These have been identified by names we use for similar concepts of our own (marriage, education, and the state, for example), or in terms of another culture where they have been identified or described (belief in mana, totemism, or shamanism), or by descriptive phrases (mother-in-law avoidance, joking relationship, or patrilocal residence). In any case, being named, a category is established, and societies can presumably be examined for the presence or absence of the named institution.

Many scholars have tried to make up lists of the institutions or customs that are found in all societies. Foremost on such lists are family, marriage, incest taboos, and division of labor by sex. Others—picked at random from scores—are games, beauty embellishments, mourning customs, joking, magic, dancing, property rights, and medical practices. These "common denominators of culture" are far less inclusive than broad encompassing patterns such as technology, social organization, or religion, but they are essentially classifications, too, with a diversified specific content. Any anthropologist working on cross-cultural material wants to know about the specific content in each culture that he is studying—he wants to know what forms of family prevail, with whom intercourse is considered incest, what work women perform, how mourning is expressed, who regularly jokes with whom—and he wants to know what the surrounding circumstances and conditions are.

In short, anthropologists are interested in the clustering of customs and associated ecologies, with the ultimate goal of saying "if this, then that." They try to discover what goes with what—for example, how patterns of subsistence, settlement, kinship, and political organization correlate. Whole cultural systems or culture types are compared for significant similarities and differences.

The anthropologist setting out to make these comparisons is problem-oriented. That is, he either seeks from the field data a hypothesis about what occurs with what, or he tests against that data a hypothesis already formulated. Two general methods of working, each with variations, are available to him.

One method is to make comparisons based on intimate knowledge—through one's own or one's colleagues' field experience—of anywhere from a few to many different cultures. These cultures may be selected from those known to be historically related, or there may be a deliberate attempt to draw examples from distinct historical traditions. Fred Eggan followed the former procedure in his study of ecology and Plains Indian social organization, as well as in his other studies of how similar American Indian cultures came to differentiate. He calls this way of working "controlled comparison" because the factors of common origin and cultural influence are known—that is, controlled—thereby throwing into relief problems of ecology and culture process. Kathleen Gough, on the other hand, felt that the conclusions in her study about the reasons for variation in the form and function of matrilineal descent systems were perhaps more valid than they would otherwise have been because her examples came from many different corners of the globe, thus avoiding the problem of cultural contamination by diffusion. Eggan controlled historical relationships by knowing about them while Gough controlled them by avoidance, through geographical selection. Other studies mix both approaches. For example, the study by Prince Peter of Greece and Denmark on polyandry—the marriage of one woman to more than one man at a time—surveys the world but draws in detail only on the Prince's own field work on related cultures in India, Ceylon, and Tibet.[2]

The other major method of comparison is to make statistical correlations of custom based on a large sample of world cultures. George Murdock, who has devoted much of his career to familiarizing himself with world ethnography and making its data easily available for cross-cultural research, initiated and continues to work according to this procedure.[3] It is increasingly used, particularly in regard to problems in social structure. For example, various students have engaged in establishing institutional correlates of in-law avoidance, cross-cousin marriage of a certain type, and matrilocal residence, to name a few. One of the most interesting of these studies, however, is concerned with culture and personality. John Whiting and Irvin Child undertook to establish correlations in seventy-five cultures between child-rearing practices and customs relating to illness.[4] Their thesis was that the nature of beliefs about the cause and treatment of illness could be predicted from data on indulgence and severity in infant care and child-training customs. For example—and this is the hypothesis for which the authors found the strongest evidence—they predicted that in societies with severe weaning practices, the adult would exhibit anxiety about oral behavior, and illness would be attributed to eating or drinking some poisonous substance or to spells cast verbally.

All of these methods of comparison have been productive, but some anthropologists have become wary about comparing institutions from culture to culture, particularly in large-scale statistical studies where there is necessarily less intimate acquaintance with the field data used. The argument is made that the interconnectedness of parts is essential to the idea of pattern in culture, and that when one part is abstracted from the whole in agreement with some outside scheme of classification—which is what a listing of institutions or customs is—damage may be done to the categories of the culture as seen from the inside. And when this part is compared with parts abstracted from still other cultures, so the reasoning goes, the possibility arises that culture elements are being compared that are not really comparable.

Controversies over definitions of institutions to be used in cross-cultural research are common in the professional journals. Questions arise, for example, about whether what is called totemism or couvade in one culture is really equivalent to a somewhat different complex of traits labelled the same thing—by outsiders—in another culture. It is also questioned whether or not particular patterns of relationships between men and women should be called marriage. No one doubts that the relationship may appropriately be called marriage whether there is one husband or wife or more than one and whether or not there are a number of other variations involving ceremony, reciprocal rights and obligations, and the status of the children. But there is a question when it comes to such marginal arrangements as those of the Nayar castes. Gough has stoutly maintained that these are marriages—to the ritual husband in the tali-tying ceremony as symbolic stand-in for potential and actual visiting husbands. Others disagree. Prince Peter, for example, has written that the visiting relationships do not come within his definition of polyandry because they are liaisons, not marriages. While some of the disagreement stems from different interpretations of the data, most of it is a matter of the definition of the social institution of marriage.

The answer to questions of definition lies in reconciling an inside view of a culture with an outside view that is not highly colored by our own cultural bias, one that is as objective as we can make it. Some anthropologists focus their interests on the *bases* for classifying culture instead of on the classifications themselves. These criteria are the non-cultural factors that are universally present in all societies, including the conditions with which each culture has had to deal and the limited resources with which it has had to work. This kind of classification has been attempted from the point of view, again, of both encompassing patterns and the finer categories, and examples of each follow.

In describing the world view of the Kota, it was remarked that they stressed man-to-man relationships, whereas the Tzotzil stressed a concern with the supernatural, which they felt to be composed of fearsome, threatening forces. In discovering the world view of any particular culture, anthropologists, following Robert Redfield's suggestion, have found it useful to think in terms of three general sets of relationships: man to nature, man to man, and man to something variously described as supernatural, ideational, or the subjective aspects of life. This three-part categorizing of culture is useful in describing a culture from the inside and, objectively, from the outside. It provides some non-cultural nails on which to hang the cultural cloaks.

Anthropologists interested in finer categories have also found culture-free referents helpful in organizing analyses of cultures for comparison. These can best be described, perhaps, as what everyman experiences: time and space, topographical features and climate, day and night, and other natural phenomena. They also include such biological universals as two sexes, long infant dependency, and different age groups. And they include social referents such as the interactions these biological universals and group living necessarily entail in the nuclear family of man, woman, and offspring, and other small groups. Thus, Whiting and Child point out in the general analysis of their data that societies everywhere, in spite of great variation in child-rearing practices and beliefs about illness, face the universal problems of infant dependency, socialization, illness, and death. This way of thinking is clarifying, and—as Whiting and Child consider it—a good point from which to start an analysis. It leads ultimately, however, straight back to the question of what to compare, since the conditions and potentials of any human society include prior cultural responses as well as culture-free referents.

Some anthropologists seek to answer the question of definitions by breaking the conventionally-designated institutions as they are variously represented in world cultures into small, more descriptive units. Thus instead of comparing societies for the presence or absence of couvade, one looks for practices concerning the father before, during, and after a birth such as food taboos, the performance of sympathetic magic to ease the birth—diving in the water or untying knots—the ritual pampering of the man as he lies in bed, or his ritual torture, and so on. Totemism, marriage, family, and government are more complex institutions, but similarly cover multiple behavior patterns that can be isolated. For example, Whiting and Child broke child-rearing practices down into those affecting five systems of behavior—oral, anal, sexual, aggressive, and dependent.

More important than this procedure, but inevitably associated with it, is distinguishing between the form and the function of any pattern of action. A function was described earlier, from the point of view of diversity, as being performed by various kinds of institutions, and interest was in the unexpected side effects of particular cultural patterns. In the context of the universal, the original idea of function is reverted to—the conception of it, that is, as answering individual and social needs, including culturally induced needs. Sustenance, shelter, sex, nurture, protection, and education, for example, are all provided by many different institutional devices. Paramount among these is the nuclear family, whether it be a single isolated unit or extended by polygamous or descent units. The family's success in this regard explains its position high on any list of universal institutions. Marriage, too, fulfills sexual, economic, and status needs, among others. The argument against calling the Nayar arrangement "marriage" centers on the fact that the status of the "husbands" does not involve economic functions. Nor, in the family, is the "father" important in the nurturing and social education of the children. This work, among the Nayar, is done by the matrilineal household groups.

So important is function in comparing cultures that Walter Goldschmidt, an anthropologist concerned with theory, has issued "a call for a comparative functionalism."[5] He suggests that anthropologists will find it more fruitful to disengage themselves from debates about definitions arising from differences in institutional form and to concern themselves instead with examining more systematically how societies have responded to certain universal needs in different circumstances and what particular needs these circumstances themselves have set in motion. He sees the social problems—not the solutions to them—as the starting point of the quest. The difficulty to be overcome, in his program, is the delineation of functions contingent on particular combinations of custom (which in turn are contingent on ecology).

Linguists, too, have been concerned about the universal as well as the unique in their particular sphere of study. The belief that language distinctively molds a people's version of reality is put in perspective by the suggestion that "what is universal in language functions much more powerfully, and in a more fundamental way, to shape men's thoughts than what is different."[6] Linguists point out that all languages are made up of the same basic elements: sounds, their meanings, and how they are put together—that is, the structure of the language. And unlike other culture elements, these have been reduced to concrete units for purposes of analysis and comparison. There are limits within which language, like the rest of culture, develops, and conditions to which it responds. Man's physical make-up limits, although within a wide range, the verbal sounds available. Bilabial and nasal classes of sounds seem to be common to all languages, as do duplications of sounds, as in baby talk. Words for "I," "you," "he," are universal, and so are personal names and terms designating kinship, gross body parts, places and topographic features, time, such processes as sleeping, eating, and dreaming, and such ideas as "not," "and," and "equal." There also seem to be common structural or grammatical problems that can be solved in only a limited number of ways, one or more of which may be used in any particular language. And whatever form a language may take, it everywhere provides symbols for thought and communication.

In summary, one approach to the quest for universals in culture sees man as faced with common problems and solving them in different ways. It further sees the solutions as being similar when conditions or limiting factors are similar, and distinct when these are different. Cross-cultural similarities are explored to discover what other cultural features and what non-cultural features are typically associated with them. The quest is for generalizations about culture type, about what kinds of solutions are produced under what conditions. In this search, anthropologists use not one but many methods of comparison. All of them suggest that what is universal in culture results from common problems and common potential.

PROCESS AND SUBSTANCE

The act of solving social problems is the dynamic aspect of the universally human. It is the process by which cultures differentiate—or perhaps become similar. The substance, the particular cultures and their distinct culture histories, is what varies. In this approach the laws of culture change are sought, and the nature of cultural evolution is explored. "If this, then that" refers, in this context, to more than correlations of cultural and other elements; it refers to causal relationships. That is to say, correlations are interpreted in terms of process. A causal relationship is said to exist when, of a set of elements or conditions regularly appearing together in world cultures, one or a combination of these elements is, just as regularly, antecedent to the others. (When the now-antecedent "this" of the formula is a single condition, it is said to be a sufficient cause, and when the "this" is more than one condition, each one is considered a necessary cause.) The quest is to discover these conditions and their sequential development.

The anthropologist intent on studying process can do so on two different levels, and there has been considerable controversy over which is the more productive procedure. One level is that of the psychological processes involved in individual behavior and group interaction; the rules sought are those governing the way man thinks—and feels—under specified conditions. Anthropologists who take this approach emphasize that culture change originates in men's minds, in individual variability, and they view physical, social, and cultural conditions as limiting, not active, causes of change. The other approach is on a more abstract level; culture histories are compared and culture traits are accounted for in terms of other culture traits. Some anthropologists who use this approach stress culture as a determining factor, evolving according to its own rules, and describe the way man thinks and feels as the consequence of culture rather than the cause of culture change. Others, however, do not view the two approaches to studying process as incompatible and shift from one level of abstraction to the other in their studies of change. Modern evolutionary theory draws heavily on both kinds of analyses.

On the psychological level, the attributes of the human mind are central to the investigation. Anthropologists stress that the human capacity to symbolize is basic to culture-making, that culture is composed of ideas which depend for formation on symbols or representations of "things"—objects or events. Each culture has its own system of symbols, but investigators believe that all individuals adjust to and change their cultures because of universal motivations and through universal mechanisms. That is, people of diverse cultures—using different symbol systems—share certain fundamental characteristics of intellect and emotion.

Primary among these characteristics are an awareness and consideration of self and an ability to identify with others and their concerns, on both conscious and unconscious levels. Some anthropologists have pointed out that "self wants," "felt needs," "incentives," or similar ideas however they are labelled, are at the root of culture change. They emphasize that these motivations, although culturally channeled and therefore various, have a universal psychic component, sometimes described as "sentiments," "drives," or "tendencies," or by some other term that implies a psychological set. And anthropologists interested in culture and personality stress that individuals everywhere adjust to conflict between their own sentiments and the values of their particular societies by mechanisms such as repression, projection, rationalization, sublimation, fixation, and so on.

Common motivations and mechanisms are explored, as they operate in various settings, under different conditions and limitations. Homer Barnett, for example, compared innovation in five cultures and one religious cult in order to find the "common conditionings and consistent mechanisms" that regularize culture change.[7] He not only describes the conditions in any society conducive to innovation—for example, an accumulation of ideas, a stimulating opposition of ideas, relative individual freedom—but he also analyzes in more detail than has any other anthropologist the individual incentives to innovate and the psychological processes involved in innovation. To be deceptively brief, he describes innovation everywhere as the result of individuals recombining, in their minds, ideas already present in the culture, substituting some for others or reorganizing them so that a qualitatively new idea—not just more of the same—emerges.

Another example of the study of process with the individual as the starting point is found in the work of Charles Erasmus.[8] In setting up what he calls a "scheme of cultural causality," he ascribes three basic motivations to all mankind—self-preservation or survival, sexual gratification, and desire for prestige. The first two are self-explanatory; the third he attributes to the pan-human social experience of enculturation. In this experience, the desire for prestige or social recognition is developed as the child, in whatever culture, comes to anticipate success or failure while learning the ways of that culture. In other words, the growing child becomes psychologically dependent on approval or regard. Erasmus suggests that man's creative, symbolizing mind, operating within the limitations of the natural and cultural environment, shapes these universal motivations into the various differentiated motivations encountered in the diverse cultures of the world.

The main thrust of his thesis is that where societies are relatively homogeneous, with little division of labor and little variety in durable goods, the prestige motivation is predominantly expressed by giving away goods rather than by accumulating them, and that where increase of food production and population density has led to the development of transportation and the use of money, and this to specialization in production and abundance of a variety of goods, the prestige motivation is predominantly expressed by owning goods. Among his examples of the first kind of society are the Siriono, where the successful hunter gives food, and the Haida of the Northwest Coast, where the potlatch was practiced. Erasmus points out variations within each type of society, and the conditions associated with them, and further describes creative or productive forms of prestige-seeking, and discusses the conditions under which these flourish.

Other approaches to understanding the process of culture change, while still on the level of individual behavior and group interaction, have a somewhat different emphasis. A sizeable group of anthropologists and other behavioral scientists have been particularly interested in studying the interaction between individuals in small groups and in particular situations to obtain more understanding of process. Some have emphasized the need for more accurate observations and quantitative measurement of interactions within such small groups as cliques, work groups, or families. (One has asserted that "the greater proportion of studies of human groups by behavioral scientists is only impressionistic and well below the standard of good novelists.")[9] Others have tried to arrive at a general logic of the interaction of individuals through analysis of the factors operating in particular situations. In the past, some cultural anthropologists have objected to what they call the reduction of cultural explanations to psychological and situational factors. In fact, most so-called purely cultural explanations assume such factors. In the quest for scientific generalizations, anthropologists attempt to make all three factors—psychological, situational, and cultural, and their interplay—explicit.

The social scientist George Homans has made some of the most systematic analyses, based on the field work of others, of how these factors work.[10] He analyzed behavior in a varied selection of small groups, classifying behavior into events, recurring events or custom, the activities group members carry on together, the interaction of these members in the process, and their sentiments. One of his selections was the family on the Pacific island of Tikopia, the data being taken from Raymond Firth's exemplary ethnography.[11] Homans' thesis is that emotional patterns in family relationships derive from the circumstances in which the family members associate, that they are not inherent in the biological connections. In Tikopia, as in many other societies throughout the world, the family was the basic sub-sistence unit, and the father directed the practical, everyday work done by its male members. The father was thus, Homans points out, in much the same position of authority over his son as are superiors over subordinates everywhere. And the son responded with respect more than with warm affection. On the other hand, the father did not direct his daughter's work, nor the mother her son's, and affection was evident in those parent-child relationships.

Homans argues that this emotional pattern tends to be present wherever the nuclear family is an important productive unit, with the father in charge of work activities, and that where the family is not such a unit and the father is not so in charge, the pattern of rela-tionship is different. He cites in evidence the Trobriand Islands, where the mother's brother was the responsible male adult and was treated with respect by the sister's son, and where the relationship between father and son, not restrained by the authority of the one over the other, was characterized by affection. He concluded that emotional ties between persons result from (are a function of) the activities they carry on together and the way the group is organized to accomplish them. For the family, "The crucial question seems to be: Is the father boss of the son?" The sentiments engendered by the situation are reinforced as they become expected behavior—that is, cultural norms. Homans further believes that if the sentiments re-sulting from interpersonal relationships are extended to associated statuses and roles, a great deal about the culture-making process has been explained.

The approach used by Homans emphasizes, in effect, the logic of the situations in which people regularly find themselves. Situational logic frequently has been invoked to make causes out of correlates. Whiting and Child, to use a familiar example, used statistical corre-lations to establish the validity of their predictions that certain child-training customs would be found to have given rise to—not just to have occurred with—certain personality types whose generalized anxieties were projected in their beliefs about the cause and treat-ment of illness. Although the authors admitted that their statistical evidence could not in itself verify their suggested causal sequence in personality development, they felt that this evidence together with the argument of plausibility—which is really the logic of the situa-tion—could verify it. But in regard to cultural development, they found that the two clusters of customs—that is, child-training and beliefs about illness—mutually reinforced each other. This finding of mutual dependence (which is what functional integration is) seems to be begging the question of causality, but from another point of view, it is not. Instead, it shifts interest in process from the level of group interaction to the long view of evolutionary trends. This level was indicated in the earlier discussion of continuity and change when ecological, historical, and functional, as well as situational factors were called upon to explain the diversification of cultures.

Modern evolutionary theory sees man as adapting, through his culture, to his total ecology. Biological evolution takes place through the natural selection of traits that have an adaptive advantage, and cultural evolution—although enormously speedier—is analogous. Neither concept, it should be emphasized, implies attaining perfection or even progress in the sense of moving toward some intrinsically valued goal. Cultural selection takes place through innovation, acceptance, and modification of culture traits and patterns. Contrary to natural selection, there is an element of choice in adaptation through cultural selection—more potential than actual as far as determining long-range results is concerned. In cultural evolution, patterns of behavior are selected in accordance with their consequences in particular cultural and ecological settings. In this sense of long-run consequences, function is causal in evolution. Mutually reinforcing customs and conflicting customs together shape the direction of cultural development. As more than one anthropologist has put it, it is a sort of "mass trial-and-error process."

Anthropologists making comparisons from society to society to shed light on how cultures develop sometimes compare cultures for similarities and differences in order to discover common origins and the diffusion of culture patterns. Thus linguists have been able to group world languages into families and characterize the "proto-" forms that gave rise to them, and other anthropologists, using archaeological, ethnographic, and historical data, have engaged in reconstructing culture history—in outlining the main form of the "tree of culture" and in drawing in detail some of its branches.[12]

Although some anthropologists have been content with the reconstruction of particular sequences of culture history, those involved in the quest for universals see this as only a preliminary step to discovering the regularities of culture change, to finding out what order there is in cultural development. To further this interest, they compare cultures for similarities and differences to establish, not historical relationships between cultures, but cross-cultural classes or typologies of cultures. In comparing types from the approach of problems and solutions, the question is, "What culture patterns are present under what conditions?" Concerning process—the solving of the problems—this question is extended to "What conditions lead to the development of what culture patterns?" It is far easier to discern ecological, historical, and functional factors operating in specific cases of differentiation—in the adaptive evolution of each unique culture, that is—than it is to abstract from these cases laws of culture change applicable generally to all cultures or to large classes of cultures.

Nevertheless, there has been an attempt to build evolutionary sequences on a worldwide scale. Here culture is seen as evolving through stages or levels of technical development in accordance with increased control of energy sources and hence of the environment. In these schemes the cumulative aspect of culture change—knowledge building upon prior knowledge—is pivotal, and because the world is the scene, diffusion is important. Most social anthropologists, however, attempt smaller-scale problems. Sometimes their hypotheses founder on so many conditional factors that the class of cultures for which the hypotheses are supposed to hold true shrinks to a negligible size. But others are "middle-range" studies, as they have been called, which gradually build a more complete understanding of culture process as they link kinds of ecologies with kinds of subsistence patterns, and these with kinds of settlement patterns, and these with types of social structure and political organization. They also later link features within each larger pattern to determine the direction of the functional relationship. For those aspects of social organization, for example, where change is not cumulative but limited to certain possibilities, students seek to generalize about what rules of residence will lead to what family groupings, kinship systems, and marriage rules, or about what systems of descent under what conditions will lead to other systems, and so on. In technical development, where the change is open-ended, they seek, for instance, to determine sequences and effects of specialization and diversification of labor.

Linguists, too, observe trends in the development of languages. There is order in the change of particular sounds to other sounds throughout a language or family of languages—called phonetic drift. Again, the change is not cumulative but limited by the possibilities. It has also been observed that, universally, words seem to narrow in meaning and depreciate in connotation far oftener than the reverse happens. It has even been suggested—and vigorously disputed—that the basic vocabularies of languages change at a rate so constant that chronologies can be established by analysis of one hundred or more words in a language.

Whether anthropologists study the process of culture-making from the vantage of individual choices and group situations or of adaptive cultural selection, they believe that the process operates everywhere on the same principles. Process and problem together explain cultural differentiation, and they also explain the convergence of culture patterns. If any pattern is found in all cultures, it is considered to be because it is adaptive in all cultures. On the other hand, if it is found only in some cultures, it is considered to be because it is adaptive to the conditions found in those cultures. The quest is to establish the range and variation of cultural behavior in relation to determining conditions.

The Primitive and the Modern

If what is universal in man's culture stems from common problems and common processes, then cultural universals are temporal, because both problems and processes can change. Man operates biologically and culturally within a range of possibilities, and as biological and cultural evolution take place through adaptation, the limits of the range change or shift. The shift in biological range cannot engage our first interest, no matter how basically important it is, because cultural adaptation has succeeded the biological in primacy for man. The shift in the cultural range is occurring at a fast pace: the label *urgent anthropology* has been placed on work to be done in some cultures, lest they disappear—unrecorded—before our eyes; and the label *urban anthropology*, to describe new studies of complex metropolitan societies, indicates the direction of the shift.

As the gamut of cultural possibilities shifts, it is conceivable that the problems common to mankind will be recast so as to transform cultural universals. The current idea of what is universal in culture coincides to a large degree with what is primitive in culture—with *primitive* used in its original sense of first, not in a sense synonymous with the non-literacy or simple technology of some contemporary peoples. It has been suggested, for instance, that the family may have originated in prehuman times, when troops of primates moved from the forests onto the plains and adapted to the competitive search for the scarce, scattered food supply there by breaking up into smaller groups consisting of one male, his females, and their young.[13] In this postulated prehistory, sex was an early basis for division of labor, with male and female specializing their tasks in the economically and sexually interdependent family. Later, techniques of cooperation, which were necessary in order to hunt down large mammals successfully, further changed the social life of man— or of the creature ancestral to man. Sharing of food among the small groups replaced competition for food, and incest taboos and taking mates from outside the immediate group set up a structure for links with other social groups through marriage and kinship ties. As the function of the family changed, so did its structure.

This speculation about primitive man includes many of the suggested cultural universals: the nuclear family, division of labor by sex, marriage, kinship, incest taboos, and cooperative groups. With the spread of mankind and cultural adaptation to specific ecological settings, primitive universals ramified into a complex and continuously changing diversity. In addition to the primitive universals, and along with proliferating versatility, similarities from culture to culture occurred. Some of these were due to common human responses to similar life situations and some were due primarily to culture contact.

The modern scene changes the context of universality and diversity in man. The distinction between historical and functional explanations of cultural development becomes more and more blurred as the cross-cultural laboratory of historically unrelated cultures disappears. Diffusion is rampant; rapid communication and transportation have all but obliterated isolated cultural development. In adding to his cultural accumulation, man increases his need to further adapt. In other words, the speeding up of the cultural process inevitably and drastically transforms the distinct ecologies to which man must continue to adapt, and it binds these ecologies into an interdependent whole. Peoples more and more share each other's culture histories, and the global net of functional relationships tightens and becomes more complex. Diversity of culture from society to society is still—and for the predictable future will remain—a dominant factor in the world, but it is increasingly accompanied by diversity of alternatives within societies, by social systems encompassing several societies, and by cross-cultural sharing of knowledge and experience by some sectors of world society.

The emerging world civilization may well change not only the details of variation but also the universally true. It is likely, for example, that the range in technologies will not only shift, but dramatically narrow, as the more primitive devices for making and doing things disappear and universally felt needs and diffusion give worldwide distribution to ever more effective devices. And other changes are likely to follow. It is conceivable, if not probable, that both the nuclear family and division of labor by sex could disappear from human culture. The primitive social situation shaped the nuclear family with its multiple functions, and as a structure it has since been efficient enough to survive—except where conditions were apparently not conducive, as among the warrior Nayar of India and in the collectives of Israel. Such exceptions are probably examples of ultraspecialized conditions and man's versatility, not harbingers of new, worldwide evolutionary adaptations. More relevant, modern urban ecologies have already led to widespread changes in the family: new needs have arisen that the family cannot fulfill, and more and more of its earlier functions have been partly shifted to other social institutions—peer groups, schools, government—and the roles of family members have altered in response. Today social and cultural conditions favoring the nuclear family and division of labor by sex still prevail. But as with other patterns of culture, this does not mean that the conditions can never change, nor that other adaptations will never appear.

The question of universal values has long interested anthropologists, as well as philosophers and other scientists. The fact that peoples of different cultures can communicate and cooperate with each other indicates that they are part of a community of shared values. All cultures have systems of morality and some values seem to be universally held. For example, everywhere survival of the society itself is valued, and various aggressive acts committed freely against people outside of the society are not committed with impunity within the society. Efforts to portray the variation that exists in ideas of the good, the true, and the beautiful, however, have been more systematic than efforts to discover what values are held in common. Value systems are represented by whole cultures, and analysis of cultures in terms of the basic principles underlying the overt behavior is one of the more difficult tasks that anthropologists have set themselves. Comparison of these principles for shared components compounds the difficulty.

A universally shared value would be presumed to have adaptive value or advantage itself. The problem of universal values, then, is sometimes couched in terms of the possibility of establishing panhuman and cross-cultural—that is, universally valid—criteria for judging particular culture patterns. In other words, how to evaluate cultures replaces the related question of what values are shared. Common processes and common problems do not mean equally successful cultural solutions. Some cultures may become so specialized in response to particular conditions that they cannot change rapidly enough to survive when those conditions change. Also, man can survive and be miserable, and some cultures seem to make people more miserable than others do. Assessments as to how well particular culture patterns fulfill individual and social needs, and how they intervene in the full satisfaction of one kind of need for the benefit of the other, are more often based on vague than on rigorously defined criteria (although they are often convincing). Nevertheless, some anthropologists feel sure that objective measurements of the "optimum functioning," "satisfaction-yield," and "grades of advance" of culture patterns beyond the technological can and will be developed.

In the meantime, ideals about individual worth and the unity of mankind spread and compete with more authoritarian and parochial values. And where such ideals are accepted rational modes of achieving them compete—without benefit of scientific measurement—with other behavior patterns. The cultural selection of these ideals and modes in adaptation to the problems inherent in an interdependent and precarious modern world would result in their becoming cultural universals. It is not inevitable, but it is conceivable.

4

The Good of Anthropology

There seems to be something of the missionary in most anthropologists. For all of their zealous quest for scientific truth, they have had reserves of enthusiasm to spend on converting people outside of the profession to an anthropological point of view, a view that values the cultural experience of others in confronting mankind's common problems. This they have done from the platform and from the printed page, in the classroom and in the civic arena. The study of man is inherently humanistic and all anthropology, in that sense, has very practical implications. The good of anthropology transcends knowledge about man and his world to encompass the uses of that knowledge in programs for the well-being of mankind.

Part of the ethical posture of all anthropologists, as represented by their professional organizations, is their intent to protect the interests of the groups that they study. This is a posture that is, in most cases, backed by a very real feeling of warm affection for the people being studied. The intent to protect is joined by a desire to help, a desire which anthropologists reconcile to varying extents with their primary goal of contributing toward a science of man. Some anthropologists have channeled their efforts more directly than others have to practical purposes, calling this segment of their work *applied, action,* or *practical anthropology.* They use their data, concepts, and techniques more systematically than others do in attempts to solve particular social, political, and economic problems that they see as connected with human welfare. In so doing, they work for particular public or private client agencies that are carrying out programs and dealing with concrete problems. These anthropologists may work for governmental agencies as consultants or as staff, or more rarely as policy-setting administrators, or they may work for industry, labor, and other groups as consultants in human relations and organization.

Applied anthropology got its original impetus from the problems of colonial administration, and the agencies that most frequently seek anthropological help are still those undertaking a program in a cross-cultural situation. The Bureau of Indian Affairs, for example, from time to time employs anthropologists, as do those governmental agencies administering overseas programs. But applied studies of communities or organizations participating in the employing agent's own general culture are also made. Whatever the respective cultural background of client or subject group, the context of the practical problems being tackled is changing communities—that is, communities either affected by or desiring developing technologies, new governmental structures, or other political, social, and economic innovations.

There used to be spirited debate between the respective advocates of pure and applied anthropology as to whether tackling specific everyday problems can enrich the science. The distinction between practical and academic problems is not so clear, however. While it is true that not all scientific propositions have immediate practical implications and not all practical problems can be usefully rephrased as scientific hypotheses, there is nevertheless enough of an overlap in the study of changing societies to have dated the debate.

Once working in particular programs, anthropologists typically see their jobs as describing the cultural matrix of particular administrative, technological, or social problems, and as predicting the effects of proposed administrative measures. They think of their role as one of enlightening the administrators, and most sharply reject critical suggestions that they are helping these administrators manipulate the people among whom they work toward certain ends. Some anthropologists in the applied field have become so sensitive to the charge of manipulation that they have deemed it beyond their office to recommend measures to administrators, as opposed to predicting the results of measures suggested by others—an oddly impractical distinction. In general, applied anthropologists are committed to specific goals only insofar as they coincide with their personal views of what is in the general interest, for the general welfare. This has left a lot of room for different ethical judgments about particular applied projects and programs.

Sensitivity to the question of ethical behavior is associated with the fact that, whatever their nature, programs have been conducted by those in power—colonial administrations for colonies, the Bureau of Indian Affairs for the Indians, the War Relocation Authority for the wartime evacuees of Japanese descent, technologically advanced nations for less developed nations, industry in regard to its labor force. Anthropology has sometimes been thought to be too closely associated with the interests of those in power. A Mexican anthropologist has noted what he calls a "conservative" tendency among applied anthropologists, a shoring up of the status quo, a misreading of the real nature of the problems of poverty, health, and human well-being.[1] Newly sophisticated African nationalists reject the notion that they need a "middleman" to interpret their cultures to others. In short, as new as the applied field is, much of its experience is already as passé as the colonies in which it originated. Recognizing this, some anthropologists have turned from oldstyle approaches to practical problems to emphasize that change introduced by fiat invites resistance, that communities must be involved in identifying their own problems and setting their own goals, and that knowledge of structure and process can be the basis for communication, cooperation, and effectiveness in achieving those goals. A few have thought that the most desirable applied work, if not the most likely to occur, is that in which the subject group and the client group are one and the same, without reference to a superordinate administrative structure. In other words, applied anthropology is turning out to have much the same message as has anthropology in general. Whether general or specific, the uses of anthropology are to better understand other people and to better understand ourselves.

Understanding Other People

Cultural relativism is the label usually given the primary anthropological perspective that recognizes that cultural diversity exists, and that sees each unique culture as having such internal coherence that particular patterns of behavior are meaningful only when considered in their total cultural context. Definitions of the good life and of the good man, according to this point of view, depend on culturally transmitted values. Morality shifts with the cultural scene. A Siriono hunter may leave his sick wife to die alone, a Plainville farmer may not; a Dahomean chief may have many wives, the Irish countryman may not; the American "organization man" may compete aggressively, the respected Hopi may not; and so on, through a long list of ways of behaving valued from place to place and time to time.

This general perspective offered by anthropology has seemed to some both obvious and sterile, but nonetheless, regardless of its limitations, it remains basic to an enlightened approach to living in a world where the physical barriers between peoples are crumbling in advance of the cultural barriers. Objections that cultural relativism, as defined here, is obvious and need no longer be emphasized are sophisticated carping, not appropriate in the face of the gross ethnocentrism of most adults and all children. Ethnocentrism projects our own culture's meanings onto patterns of behavior occurring in completely different cultural contexts. It is not easy to avoid doing this without some background in how and why cultures differ, in the objective facts about man and culture that make up the body of anthropological knowledge.

The question of the sterility of a culturally relative point of view, in the practical and not the scientific sense, is a more complicated one because it goes beyond the objective facts about diversity and the integration of culture and asks how we judge these facts, how they affect our attitudes. In the view of some critics of cultural relativism, cultural explanations of such customs as human sacrifice, cannibalism, slavery, and so on, are seen as momentarily interesting but in the long run irrelevant, because nothing will make us like these things. It is true that, for example, the explanation concerning the sacrifice of thousands by an incoming Dahomean king upon the death of his king-father that it was "a touching instance of the king's filial piety, deplorably mistaken, but perfectly sincere," leaves us, actually, very untouched. Neither do we find attractive such cultural habits as using one's ancestors' skulls for curative purposes, cutting off one's wife's nose for adultery, and so on. Not only do we abhor certain customs, but whole peoples may arouse our dislike. Ethnographers are notoriously partisan about "their" people, but not always. As one anthropologist succinctly commented, ". . .there are societies continued contact with which merely results in increasing dislike."

We do constantly make judgments about cultures and peoples and undoubtedly are most comfortable when making them from the vantage of an unenlightened ethnocentrism. Understanding—which means knowing the reasons for, and does not mean liking or accepting—mitigates our judgments because it acknowledges that the unique takes place only in the framework of a shared humanity. In a sense, we ourselves become associated with what we are judging. This kind of understanding does not in itself solve any problems about how to act in the face of culture patterns we find distressing, but it does provide the essential foundations of fact for deciding upon action. Cultural relativism, far from being a sterile perspective, when joined with a perspective that recognizes the unity of mankind can be productive of progress toward evolving universally humane goals. Our problem is neither how to like each other nor how to be all alike; it is how to live together with regard for others' individual and social potential in the close-knit world of today.

The general good of anthropology in understanding other people is this affecting of attitudes by the knowledge of facts. In special instances, applied anthropologists can be helpful to those trying to introduce technological or social change—practices relating to improved diet, agriculture, or education, for example—in particular cultures by pointing out the ways that each of these cultures is integrated, by suggesting how the proposed change may have unlooked for, perhaps undesired, results, and by clarifying the social organization so that communication and cooperation between program administrators and people can be effected.

There is now, and for the foreseeable future, the need to understand the extent to which cultures are unique, to explore the different backgrounds of both old and newly emerging nations, as well as of small groups still relatively remote from the modern scene. Cultures differ from each other in varying degrees, however. Cross-cultural situations can be defined within modern heterogeneous societies as well as from society to society. In the United States, to name only the more obvious examples, there is considerable cultural variety from South to North, from East to West, from Megalopolis to Appalachia, and from generation to generation. Nevertheless, the variation is not so great but that we are aware of sharing many culture patterns. In this general sense of diminishing cultural differences, other people become ourselves.

Understanding Ourselves

Cultural relativism clears away misconceptions about the nature of man in culture and indicates a wider potentiality than we would otherwise be aware of, so that we can see what is common to all mankind due to his biological unity and his pan-human experience. In understanding other cultures we try to look beyond customs that to us are strange, even shocking, and see recognizable people in recognizable situations doing recognizable things; our first effort is to get an inside view of the culture. In understanding ourselves, we try to take an outsider's view and look at even our most ingrained social habits dispassionately (although a few anthropologists take an op-

posite tack and write what one of them has called a "passionate ethnography" of contemporary American culture). Alerted to the order
and variation in human behavior by the study of other cultures, we
can see our own behavior as molded by our particular culture history,
our own customs as functionally integrated, and our own society as
organized by status into social groups and sectors and ongoing systems. Such cool awareness of how our culture is patterned and how
our society works stems directly from comparing the customs and
institutions of others. The classic expression of this perspective is
Clyde Kluckhohn's—"Anthropology holds up a great mirror to man
and lets him look at himself in his infinite variety."[2]

We understand ourselves not only by the contrasts and similarities that we see in this mirror but also by studying ourselves in the
same way that we study others. Anthropological concepts and method are basically as applicable to modern societies as they are to the
traditional societies most often associated with the discipline, as the
steadily increasing number of volumes of community and regional
studies by anthropologists and field-working sociologists attests. The
change of scene from the exotic to the familiar presents the worker
with new problems—and solves some old ones—but the general out-
line of field procedure is the same. And although the introduction of
urban complexity requires sharpening of techniques and ideas, the
tools are the ones that were forged in the study of simpler societies.

The same concepts and methods are also applicable to particular
segments of a society, or to systems operating within the larger social system. Anthropologists have studied patterned social behavior
in such diverse American loci as hospitals, factories, families, and
bars. Perhaps the most appropriate illustration of such application of
anthropological perspectives, however, is one suggested in the introduction of this book—that is, looking at education anthropologically.
In studying other cultures, anthropologists have long specialized in
problems of teaching and learning, problems that are inherent in
consideration of the life cycle and rites of passage from birth to death,
the processes and institutions of enculturation, the effect of culture
on personality formation, and culture change. It is not surprising,
therefore, that some anthropologists have turned their attention to
the study of our schools as primary institutions for transmitting
culture and as important sources of culture modification. To date,
only a handful of scholars have seriously researched modern American educational problems from an anthropological point of view,
but their findings indicate a rich lode to be mined, to the benefit of education and anthropology alike.

Students from both fields are joining forces to collect field data on what is actually happening in the classroom, the school, and the school community, and to analyze this data in terms of a series of concepts or specific problems. These "ethnographies of the classroom" or descriptions of "the culture of schools," as they have been called, are expected to form the bedrock upon which a solid, comparative educational anthropology can be built.

Current efforts and interests include two general approaches. Some students concentrate on the micro-society of the classroom, trying to look beyond the conventional activities there to see behavior patterns related to different past experiences of pupils and teachers, and to observe how new patterns evolve or old ones are reinforced. Others widen their focus to envelop the whole school system or school community, attempting to unravel its complexity by tracing the many interconnections of its component parts. Whether the narrower or the broader approach is taken, investigators are interested in a wide variety of central issues.

Paramount among these, although most difficult to deal with objectively, are values and goals in school education. In particular, the examination of stated goals of mass public education against a background of unstated but nonetheless real values and assumptions can throw into relief means of achieving alternative or even competing virtues—for example, those methods used to instill democratic attitudes and those which foster various kinds of elitism. More important, the sifting of underlying values that are being acted upon from ideal ones that are being talked about can provide a measure for appraisal of both educational procedures in the classroom and the social organization of the whole school.

Anthropologists are interested in both the formal and informal structure of the schools—the cliques as well as the clubs, and coffee time in the teachers' lounge as well as meetings of the school board—because such social institutions give the clue to how the system really works. Observation of interpersonal relations in face-to-face groups yields the primary data with which a total picture can be constructed of how particular groupings, events, or activities affect one another and the educational process itself. When the purposes of a variety of school institutions—honor societies, assemblies, and student government, for example—are examined against knowledge of how they function in other ways in the system as a whole, we may get some fresh looks at old habits. From this same kind of data, viewed over time, insights can be gained about the schools as a force for stability and a field for innovation.

An important part of looking at education anthropologically is examining the roles of the various status sectors within the schools, both objectively, from the outside, and from the inside, which is more difficult. How the administrators, teachers, other school personnel, students, and parents typically view their own and the others' roles and how each group defines the school situation are particularly important in understanding conflict and the exercise of power in school communities. So, too, are systematic studies of the interaction between school and other social and cultural systems in the wider community, including the political, and of behavior patterns related to subcultural status due to national, class, religious, or racial origin. (The prefix in *subcultural* simply indicates that the cultural entity is part of an encompassing culture and does not refer to evaluation of culture content.)

Teachers may well desire that conclusions and recommendations stem from such research, and be disappointed that it has not yet yielded a systematic body of knowledge, based on broadly collected field data, that can be picked over for solutions to specific problems. However, the anthropologists' experience carries to teachers the more general message of understanding other groups, a message that is widely applicable precisely because of its general nature. The anthropologist Paul Bohannon has given a unique version of this message in an article in which he draws an analogy between the work of field anthropologists and classroom teachers.[3] Both groups, he points out, must work with their whole personalities to gain acceptance in their "communities," to be able to communicate with the people they are working with, so that they can get the job done. They must be participants in what is going on, but at the same time they must be able to draw back and observe what is going on objectively. This detachment-within-involvement has to come not only from an attempt to understand the internal attitudes and outer patterns of the group concerned, but also from an awareness of one's own feelings, values, and assumptions, and of the ways that they are manifested.

In summary, participant observation, analysis, and comparison are methods, and pattern, value, structure, function, and process are concepts, with which we can try to understand ourselves in our own school systems just as we try to understand other people in other social systems. No other effort is more crucial, for on our understanding rests our performance, and on our performance rests the future.

Notes

2. The Diversity of Cultures

1. John Ross, *A Voyage of Discovery*, Vol. I (London: J. Murray, 1819).

2. Allan Holmberg, *Nomads of the Long Bow* (Washington, D.C.: Smithsonian Institution, 1950).

3. For the Haida as an example, see George P. Murdock, *Our Primitive Contemporaries* (New York: The Macmillan Company, 1936), pp. 221–261, and *Culture and Society* (Pittsburgh, Pa.: University of Pittsburgh Press, 1965), pp. 262–293. For a description of potlatch among the Kwakiutl, see Ruth Benedict, *Patterns of Culture* (New York: Penguin Books, 1946), pp. 160–205.

4. E. Adamson Hoebel, "The Nature of Culture," in Harry L. Shapiro (ed.), *Man, Culture, and Society* (New York: Oxford University Press, 1960), pp. 179–180.

5. Jules Henry, *Jungle People* (New York: Vintage Books, 1964).

6. See Robert Redfield, *The Little Community* (Chicago: The University of Chicago Press, 1960), pp. 132–137, for a relevant discussion, in regard to the different views he and Oscar Lewis had of life in Tepoztlan, Mexico.

7. Henry, *op. cit.*, p. 46.

8. James West, *Plainville, U.S.A.* (New York: Columbia University Press, 1945).

9. Waldemar Bogoras, *The Chukchee*, The Jesup Expedition, VII (New York: G. E. Stechert and Co., 1904–1909), 359.

10. Bronislaw Malinowski, *Coral Gardens* (London: G. Routledge and Sons, 1929).

11. Harold C. Conklin, *Hanunóo Agriculture,* FAO Forestry Development Paper No. 12 (Rome: Food and Agriculture Organization of the United Nations, 1957).

12. David Mandelbaum, "The World and the World View of the Kota," in McKim Marriott (ed.), *Village India* (Chicago: University of Chicago Press, 1955).

13. Calixta Guiteras Holmes, *Perils of the Soul* (New York: The Free Press, 1961).

14. John Seeley, R. A. Sim, and Elizabeth Loosely, *Crestwood Heights* (New York: Basic Books, Inc., Publishers, 1956).

15. Dorothy Lee, *Freedom and Culture* (Englewood Cliffs, N. J.: Prentice-Hall, Inc., 1959), p. 130.

16. Lauriston Sharp, "Steel Axes for Stone Age Australians," in E. H. Spicer (ed.), *Human Problems in Technological Change* (New York: Russell Sage Foundation, 1952).

17. Clyde Kluckhohn and Dorothea Leighton, *The Navaho* (Chicago: University of Chicago Press, 1946).

18. Alfred Kroeber and Clyde Kluckhohn, *Culture: A Critical Review of Concepts and Definitions* (New York: Vintage Books, 1963). Discussion about certain aspects of the meaning of *culture* has continued until some few despair of any agreed upon precision and propose quite seriously to drop the word entirely.

19. Kathleen Gough, "Nayar: Central Kerala," in David M. Schneider and Kathleen Gough (eds.), *Matrilineal Kinship* (Berkeley, Calif.: University of California Press, 1961).

20. Francis Hsu, *Clan, Caste and Club* (New York: D. Van Nostrand Co., Inc., 1963).

21. Conrad Arensberg, *The Irish Countryman* (Gloucester, Mass.: Peter Smith, 1959); Conrad Arensberg and Solon T. Kimball, *Family and Community in Ireland* (Gloucester, Mass.: Peter Smith, 1961).

22. Sharp, *op. cit.*

23. Margaret Mead, "Our Educational Emphases in Primitive Perspective," in George D. Spindler (ed.), *Education and Culture* (New York: Holt, Rinehart & Winston, 1963), p. 311.

24. Cora Du Bois, *The People of Alor* (Minneapolis, Minn.: University of Minnesota Press, 1944).

25. Laurence Wylie, *Village in the Vaucluse* (New York: Harper & Row, 1964).

26. Herbert Gans, *Urban Villagers* (New York: The Free Press, 1962).

27. A. Irving Hallowell, *Culture and Experience* (Philadelphia, Pa.: University of Pennsylvania Press, 1955), p. 351.

28. Spindler, *op.cit.*, pp. 24 – 26.

29. Art Gallaher, Jr., *Plainville Fifteen Years Later* (New York: Columbia University Press, 1961).

30. Fred Eggan, *The American Indian* (Chicago: Aldine Publishing Company, 1966).

3. The Universally Human

1. Robert Redfield, "The Universally Human and the Culturally Variable," in Margaret Park Redfield (ed.), *Human Nature and the Study of Society* (Chicago: University of Chicago Press, 1962), pp. 439 – 452.

2. H.R.H. Prince Peter of Greece and Denmark, *A Study of Polyandry* (The Hague: Mouton and Co., 1963).

3. For details, see George P. Murdock, "Cross-Cultural Sampling," *Ethnology*, V (January, 1966), 97 – 114, and "Ethnographic Atlas: A Summary," *Ethnology*, VI (April, 1967), 109 – 169.

4. John Whiting and Irvin Child, *Child Training and Personality* (New Haven, Conn.: Yale University Press, 1953).

5. Walter Goldschmidt, *Comparative Functionalism* (Berkeley, Calif.: University of California Press, 1966).

6. Joseph Casagrande, "Language Universals in Anthropological Perspective," in Joseph Greenberg (ed.), *Universals of Language* (Cambridge, Mass: M.I.T. Press, 1963), p. 231.

7. Homer Barnett, *Innovation: The Basis of Cultural Change* (New York: McGraw-Hill Book Company, 1953).

8. Charles Erasmus, *Man Takes Control* (New York: The Bobbs-Merrill Co., Inc., 1961).

9. F. L. W. Richardson, Jr., "Recollecting vs. 'Live' Recording: Organizational Relationships of a Surgeon," *Human Organization*, 25, (Summer, 1966), 163.

10. George Homans, *The Human Group* (New York: Harcourt, Brace & World, Inc., 1950).

11. Raymond Firth, *We, the Tikopia* (London: Allen and Unwin, 1957).

12. As described by Ralph Linton in *The Tree of Culture* (New York: Vintage Books, 1959), p. v., this tree resembles the banyan tree of the tropics, whose branches from the parent trunk interjoin to give rise to supporting trunks, spreading and growing until, although still a single plant, it looks like a miniature jungle.

13. Bernard Campbell, *Human Evolution* (Chicago: Aldine Publishing Company, 1966), p. 280.

4. The Good of Anthropology

1. Guillermo Bonfil Batalla, "Conservative Thought in Applied Anthropology: A Critique," *Human Organization*, 25 (Summer, 1966), 89–92.

2. Clyde Kluckhohn, *Mirror for Man* (New York: McGraw-Hill Book Company, 1949), p. 11.

3. Paul Bohannon, "Field Anthropologists and Classroom Teachers," *Social Education*, 32, (February, 1968), 161–166.

Index